THE POWER OF CREATIVITY

LEARNING HOW TO BUILD LASTING HABITS, FACE YOUR FEARS AND CHANGE YOUR LIFE (BOOK 1)

BRYAN COLLINS

BECOME A *Writer* TODAY

CONTENTS

For A.

By Bryan Collins

Become a Writer Today

PREFACE

This book is just one of a popular three-part series that will teach you how to become more creative and find better ideas.

Visit
becomeawritertoday.com/poc

Visit becomeawritertoday.com/poc and I'll send you book two free today.

1

THE MIRROR

"We don't see things as they are, we see them as we are."
– Anais Nin

OCTOBER 17TH, 2009

It was the morning after my thirtieth birthday party, and I was lying on the cold tiles in the upstairs bathroom of my house. My skin felt sticky to touch, and I imagined a shard of glassware was tearing my head in two.

I got up, put my hands on the sink, looked in the mirror and into my bloodshot eyes. I didn't like what I saw.

I could (almost) forgive myself for having a crippling hangover the morning after my birthday. I knew my life had some trappings of success: a healthy son and daughter, a wife, a paying job and a modest-sized house.

But I knew I was a failure.

However, since I was a five-year-old boy reading a tattered copy of Roald Dahl's *The BFG* underneath the bedcovers with a flashlight between my teeth, I wanted to be a writer. But to want something and to be brave enough to pursue it are two different things. I'd spent 25 years being too afraid to pursue what I wanted.

For years, I read books about getting more done, coming up with ideas, unlocking fresh thinking, changing habits, writing, and managing To Do lists, calendars and even time itself, but I was the ultimate procrastinator.

I collected other people's big ideas like they were rare coins that belonged in a glass case at the back of my mind. I never put what I found into practise. I was too afraid to start, too afraid to go after what I wanted, too afraid to think big.

Sure, some of my decisions opened doors for me. I talked about Ernest Hemingway and Anaïs Nin over pints of beer with friends, and I studied journalism in college (a suitable course for any would-be writer). I even talked my way into a job as a print journalist for a Dublin newspaper.

There, I was paid to report on news stories each week. I was terrible at it. I dreaded the weekly news meetings, and I couldn't stand being in the same room as the editor of the newspaper. I was permanently devoid of ideas to write or report on, and everybody at the paper knew it.

I didn't last long at that job or the next job in the media.

I left journalism and drifted into another career that had nothing to do with writing, a career that snuffed out any sparks of creativity from its employees with mind-numbing routines, policies and procedures.

I became afraid of taking creative chances because I was worried about paying the bills and of what others would think. I became caught up in the day-to-day practicalities of life.

So the morning after my birthday, I looked in the mirror at my receding hairline and the first flecks of grey in my beard. I saw I was no closer to becoming a writer than the five-year-old boy who stayed up at night reading a frayed, yellow copy of *The BFG*.

I realised I needed to face my fears. I was a zebra who needed to change his stripes.

I needed to at least start, and I could do it with small, incremental changes. I'd work on becoming physically and mentally healthier. I'd seek out new ideas and put them into practise. I'd get over feeling afraid of rejection and failure, and I'd learn the demands of my craft.

The Road Ahead

To be creative is to embark on a long journey. I can't promise where you'll end up, but I know where we'll start. In this book, I'll explain why keeping an orderly and quiet life will help you prepare for fantastic and wild ideas.

I'll also guide you through setting up your studio or where you work for success, the difference between efficiency and effectiveness and how to feed your subconscious.

You'll discover why knowing your guiding purpose is just as important as feeling inspired about your creative projects. You'll learn how a mentor can help you face your fears and overcome everyday obstacles. And you'll find out what to do if you can't find one.

I cannot think of anything more powerful for writers, musicians or artists than a daily creative habit. So, I'll guide you through which ones to cultivate and what to ignore.

I'll explain why strengthening your mind and body and working hard is key to fresh thinking. But what if you're feeling exhausted?

Well, you can always turn to one of your side projects like television director, producer and writer Matthew Weiner, which I'll explain later.

Finally, we'll go to war. We're going to conquer any fears you have about creativity or your craft and then move boldly forward.

In each chapter, I'll draw on scientific studies (because we can all benefit from a little science), and I'll also examine the lives of contemporary and past creative masters from the arts, business, technology and more.

Each chapter concludes with applicable exercises or "Creative

Takeaways" that will help you overcome common setbacks in your work.

(Because, hey, theory is nice, but practise is better.)

Who This Book is For

It's the first in a three-part series about creativity, which I wrote for new writers, musicians, filmmakers, and artists.

This book, in particular, is for anyone who has ever thought "I have a hard time being creative" or "I would like to discover my passion" or even "the prospects of my work being rejected is terrifying".

If you're an artist adrift, I wrote this book for you.

I'm not all sunshine, rainbows and lollipops, so if you're looking for a shortcut to a six-figure paycheque or a glittering review in the *New Yorker*, get out now.

I'd love a shortcut as much as the next person, you will find none here. You're still going to have to do the hard work. As I've learned firsthand, when your eyes are bloodshot, your fingers callused and your back aching, you're still on the hook for working on your ideas, for stepping forwards.

Oh, and here's the thing:

When I read books that tackle subjects like creativity, I'm struck by how distant the writer is from his or her research, and how dry the material reads.

It's as if a SERIOUS topic like creativity warrants objective distance and emotional detachment. Yet, reader loses when an author's detachment results in dry prose devoid of storytelling and steeped in research and critical analysis.

Regardless of whether the material between the covers is worth the slog, those books are just not much fun to read.

I don't want you to lose.

So you'll find my story, my fears, my struggles, my wins and my setbacks woven through these pages. I've put as much of myself and as many illuminating stories about habit-building, conquering your fears and nurturing your creativity into this book as possible.

But, you've been waiting long enough.

So, let's begin.

2

PREPARE TO BE INSPIRED

*"I think people who create and write, it actually does flow - just flows from
into their head, into their hand, and they write it down. It's simple."*
– Paul McCartney

I DREAM of standing on the Cliffs of Moher, edging towards the
Atlantic Ocean, the wind snapping at my skin. I dream of being
surrounded by friends and family and then falling until I'm over-
whelmed by the raging sea.

I dream of a restaurant lit by candles, of medium-rare filet steak,
dark red Bordeaux and marijuana. I dream of eating with friends
from college and us realising we have nothing to share anymore.

I dream of returning to my old job as a care worker in a hospital,
being pulled aside by my ageing manager – her curly brown hair now
straight and grey – and being told, "You don't know how to do this
anymore Bryan, you're fired."

I dream of producing a radio show for a would-be politician and
then being let go. I dream about falling forwards and of reinvention.

I dream of lying in bed next to a warm body and telling her my
problems. I dream of her hands moving across the dark, of being
touched and being unable to touch. I dream of standing at the top of

a church putting a ring on her finger. I dream of marriage and divorce, of regret and of yesterday.

I dream of a sunny October morning, the day of the Dublin City Marathon and of being unable to find the start line. I dream of putting one foot in front of the other even though my muscles are on fire; I dream of running on until I reach the finish line.

I dream of wearing a new grey suit, of tall glass buildings in the city, of shaking my new boss's hand and starting again. I dream of six-figure paydays, of sham and drudgery, and financial ruin.

I dream of melting clocks, war, fog and smoke, steel tipped helmets and marching black leather boots, my bloody face in the dirt. I dream of holding the line. I dream of a cold Christmas morning. I wake up covered in sweat.

I've got an idea.

An Artist's Slumber

In 2008, a British radio presenter asked Paul McCartney (b. 1942) to name his favourite Beatles song. McCartney answered that he loves "Yesterday", which he recorded in 1965.

 One of mine? If I had to answer one song, it would have to be 'Yesterday' because it came to me in a dream and because 3,000 people are supposed to have recorded it.
That was entirely magical – I have no idea how I wrote that. I just woke up one morning and it was in my head. I didn't believe it for about two weeks."

Oh to sit around on the couch or lie in bed, waiting for a divine moment of inspiration to strike. Then to rush downstairs, open a notebook and bash out 10,000 words of great prose that sets the world on fire or, as in McCartney's case, scratch out a hit record that becomes the most covered song of all time.

McCartney isn't the first creative master to turn towards dreams for inspiration.

Spanish surrealist painter Salvador Dali (1904-1989) – he of the narrow, upright moustache – slept as deeply and as soundly as possible before working on his big ideas.

Dali depended on "physical and psychic calm" that a deep, restful night's sleep brought before approaching the white, virgin canvas and beginning a new pictorial work.

He even went as far as to influence his dreams by having a valet pour fragrances on his pillow before waking, having melodies play quietly in the background as he slept and applying intense light to his pupils so he could dream in colours.

In his book, *50 Secrets of Magic Craftsmanship,* Dali wrote to aspiring painters:

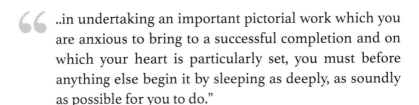

> ..in undertaking an important pictorial work which you are anxious to bring to a successful completion and on which your heart is particularly set, you must before anything else begin it by sleeping as deeply, as soundly as possible for you to do."

After a deep night's sleep, Dali worked each morning for several hours on his surrealist paintings of melting pocket watches, distorted faces, landscapes and dream sequences.

When afternoon came, Dali returned to his subconscious mind for inspiration. He sat in a bony Spanish armchair near his painting supplies, tilted his head back and draped his hands over the arms of the chair.

In his left hand, Dali held a large heavy key, which he dangled over a plate on the floor.

As soon as Dali closed his eyes and fell asleep, his grip relaxed, he dropped the key and it landed on the plate. The crashing sound woke him, and he immediately picked up his painting supplies and recommenced painting while in a dream-like state.

Dali explained,

 And the most characteristic slumber, the one most

appropriate to the exercise of the art of painting . . . is the slumber which I call 'the slumber with a key,'...you must resolve the problem of 'sleeping without sleeping,' which is the essence of the dialectics of the dream, since it is a repose which walks in equilibrium on the taut and invisible wire which separates sleeping from waking."

At first glance, stories like these give the illusion of the creative process being quick and easy and altogether alien from the grind and monotony of daily hard work.

Look more closely at these moments of inspiration, and you'll discover idling about or waiting until an idea arrives is not how masterpieces get made.

Creative masters like McCartney and Dali are able to recognise inspiration and then act on it only because they've spent hours turning up and doing the work beforehand.

They've fertilised the soil and seeded their ideas long in advance. Such masters are intimately familiar with the tools of their craft, and they've spent time shaping fragile concepts of big ideas.

In an interview with *Paste Magazine*, McCartney said,

> [Songs] definitely just arrive out of thin air, but I think you have to know how to spot them. I think someone building a car suddenly knows when the design is right or when the engine sounds good. After a while you get used to that, and you say, 'Yeah, this is the way you go.'"

McCartney doesn't just wait for ideas for hit songs to appear out of thin air. He also gets ideas for song hooks by constantly considering how others compose and then by developing his idea to spot those hooks in the wild.

> As far as hooks are concerned, I must say I just love them. I love them on other people's records. I love it.

You find yourself whistling it or wake up thinking, 'What's that? Oh, I love that. What is it?' The best scenario is when you realize it's one of yours. 'Oh, it's the one I'm writing currently.' That's the right sign. But I tell you what, it beats working."

In Dali's book referenced above, he provides new artists with a schedule they must follow.

If you're wrestling with an idea for a masterpiece, he recommends turning up before the virgin canvas each morning at eight o'clock and working for at least five and a half hours, six days a week until your masterpiece is complete.

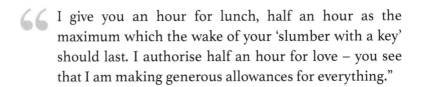 I give you an hour for lunch, half an hour as the maximum which the wake of your 'slumber with a key' should last. I authorise half an hour for love – you see that I am making generous allowances for everything."

Dali continues:

I guarantee you that if with the five and a half hours that I give you to fill in the landscape or sea you do not have enough...you are not the great painter of genius that you claim to be and your work will not be the masterpiece we expected from your brush."

For McCartney and Dali, the creative process is as much about preparation and good habits as it is about moments of inspiration.

Creative masters keep a schedule, they treat their work seriously, and get to it whether they're inspired or not. You too can cultivate creative habits that change your life, and here's how.

Sacrifice the Non-Essentials

So you want to build lasting habits that change your life?

Well, you might enjoy sitting down on the couch each evening to watch a comedy or a film or even play a video game, but now things are different. You will replace old habits with productive activities.

You won't have as much free time as you used too. You must commit to spending some of your free hours alone in your room or studio, even if a boss or lover wants to know what you're doing.

Are you prepared to sacrifice watching television, playing games, spending time on social media, reading trashy books, enjoying late nights out or pursuing side projects that have nothing to do with your creative passions?

Because when you sacrifice the non-essential parts of your day, you'll gain the momentum you need to progress your big ideas.

Tame Your Environment

If you're not in the habit of keeping a creative schedule, you'll encounter mental resistance when you try to do your work. Go easy on yourself by setting up an office or studio with mental triggers.

Remove anything from this environment that distracts, for example, television or a games console. You could even go as far as disconnecting Internet access in advance.

Willpower is a finite resource, and you don't want to expend it wrestling with distractions.

Remove anything from your environment that has nothing to do with your big ideas. Leave visual clues about your work and ideas. Write notes to yourself each night about what to work on the next day.

Ease Yourself into It

To cultivate lasting creative habits, prepare your work in advance.

This practice ensures starting work each day takes a minimum amount of effort.

If you're writing a book chapter, for example, open the chapter in your computer, connect your headphones and queue your writing music in advance. This way, upon waking each morning, you'll know what to do immediately without thinking about it.

You can also ease yourself in by spending 10 or 15 minutes reviewing the previous day's work, reading, doodling or admiring the work of others who inspire you.

Like stretches help an athlete warm up, this will help you become more intimate with your ideas faster.

Create Space

Working on your big ideas can be messy, but you need a clear space to create this mess in the first place.

When you finish working for the day, reset your workspace and sort through what you've worked on. Just as a master craftsman puts away his tools after work, you must tidy your desk or studio, file your notes and reorganise everything.

Then, lay out the following day's work and ideas and the tools you need before you go to bed.

Become More Efficient

The creative process is sometimes sloppy and disorganised.

Both good ideas and bad ideas appear at unusual times like at 03:23. They arrive in unexpected places too, like in the shower. So, you must be efficient about your routine.

To do this, anticipate what you need and then arrange everything so it's to hand. Organise your tools and your supplies so that everything is in one place that you can easily access.

Then, check that you have everything you need such as pens, pencils, paints, paper, books, your notes, a firm resolve etc. before you start working.

You don't want to waste time looking for your notes, research or buying supplies online when you could be working on a big idea.

Become More Effective

Dali recommends artists set a goal of painting their masterpiece by working six days a week, but what if this practice is too ambitious?

Open up your calendar, set a deadline for your creative project and, working backwards, block out time on your calendar each day to create. Then hold yourself accountable to this routine.

At the end of the week or month, review your routine. Ask yourself how many new ideas you came up with and whether you're hitting your target word count or putting in enough hours in front of the canvas or page.

If you find your creative project isn't on track, consider what's holding you back and how you can remove these blocks. Get outside help from somebody who will hold you accountable if you must. Only renegotiate your deadlines as a last resort.

Nudge Yourself Along

If you can't write for an hour today, sit down and write for 15 minutes. If you don't have enough energy to paint or write after work, try for just five minutes in the morning.

If you're feeling anxious about emailing interview requests for your documentary, just draft the email and gather the addresses you need.

If you're a writer, turn up in front of the blank page at the same time every day and force yourself to write even if you've got nothing to say. I like to start with a short journal entry about my intentions for the day or re-read the previous day's work.

If you're a filmmaker, go to the set or your script and figure out how you're going to approach the next scene in a fresh way.

You will make steady but determined progress towards your goal if you nudge your big ideas along in some small way each day.

Feed Your Subconscious

Before I go to bed, I read a section of what I worked on that day. I hold this thought in my mind for a few seconds before going to sleep. I do this because keeping an idea in my mind passes it over to my subconscious, which will continue to work on the idea while I sleep.

When I wake the next morning, I try to remember what I dreamt. I write this down quickly before it disappears from my mind.

Afterwards, I make a conscious effort to get to do at least an hour's work before I eat and get ready for the day, as I want to catch the ideas of my subconscious while they linger and before the demands of the day take over.

If you're going to use this approach, hold an image of what you want to accomplish firmly in your mind before you drift to sleep. It should be something specific, like a particular section of your book or a verse in a song you're writing.

Reward Yourself

The Hindu spiritual text, the Bhagavad Gita tells us, "You have the right to work, but never to the fruit of work. You should never engage in action for the sake of reward, nor should you long for inaction."

So, it's no surprise that creative masters feel motivated to continue even if they're working alone or progress is slow.

One of the best ways to foster this inner motivation is to mark small victories, like keeping a new creative routine or reaching a little milestone such as a targeted word-count or a finished painting.

You can mark these milestones by taking a trip to a museum, a walk in the park, a lie in on the weekends or by enjoying a night out with friends.

The goal here isn't to work on an idea solely for a reward; it's to build a mental link between your new creative routine and positive experiences.

Commit to Your Ideas

You can't count on creativity to appear at will; it takes months or even years to develop the mental resources you need to come up with or recognise quality ideas consistently, but here's the thing:

Turning up every day sends a signal to your subconscious that you're dedicated to the virgin canvas, the blank page or your medium of choice.

Like a long-distance runner training for the Olympics, by turning up each day, you prepare your mind and body for your creative, hard work.

Then, when an idea arrives in a dream or when inspiration strikes, you'll have the resources to recognise it and act on it like McCartney and Dali.

Creative Takeaways

- Sleep deeply before you approach the blank page or the canvas.
- Remember, you must find it easy to begin your creative practise, and it should feel effective, efficient and rewarding (at least some of the time) if it's going to become a habit.

3

TRACE YOUR CREATIVE ROOTS

"The function of education is to teach one to think intensively and to think critically. Intelligence plus character – that is the goal of true education."
– Martin Luther King Jr.

PAY THE BILLS, feed your family, exercise, meditate, paint, draw, play music, learn to cook, speak Spanish, travel to Peru, spend six months teaching English in Southeast Asia, record an album, craft artisanal clay pots, photograph your muse, study for an MBA, start a blog.

You could spend your life on thousands of worthwhile creative endeavours.

The painful realities of life complicate your ability to do what you want. And your options narrow the older you get.

If you want to become a more successful creative person, you will face tough decisions about what you'd like to do (like spending six months teaching English or travelling around Peru) and what you must do (compose an album, write a novel, etc).

Talent, opportunity and riches aren't enough. Talented artists might get off the starting blocks quicker than the rest of us, but their talents are of little use without an idea of where they're going.

The rich artist or the artist with more opportunities than his or her peers might be able to create flashier works than others (at least at first), but he or she will squander their talents or garb themselves in the "Emperor's New Clothes" unless they know what it's all for.

If you don't know where you're going, the current of life will sweep you along like an object afloat in a river, sometimes dashing you against the rocks and sometimes holding you back in a sluggish stream.

Your only real choice is to cast a rudder into the river, and while you're unable to control the current, you can at least steer your humble craft in the right direction.

Your Guiding Purpose

I once spent a year unemployed.

I was in a secure job that paid relatively well, but it was awful. When I couldn't stand the thought of staying even one more day, I broke from this job and found work as a press officer for a charity. It was supposed to be my dream job, but after several months my manager let me go.

He told me I didn't have what it takes. I contacted my old employer and asked for my job back, but I'd already burned the boats; there was no way I could return to my old and safe role.

I spent months out of work, considering what career I should follow. I knew I wanted to write, but I didn't know if this meant working in journalism, public relations or some other career.

I was adrift.

I eventually discovered people who are happy in their chosen professions face these types of crises armed with a personal mission statement, a guiding purpose or code.

They have done the hard work of educating themselves about what drives and inspires them. They know, too, that creativity doesn't just appear at will. It takes months and years of hard and purposeful work.

Originally from Chicago, singer and poet Patti Smith (b. 1946) has dedicated her life to the pursuit of art through poetry and punk rock. During the 1970s, she began performing poetry in clubs around New York and teaching herself how to play the guitar.

At first, Smith played alone in her room before performing for friends and then reciting poetry in small New York clubs.

Finally, she embraced the guitar and the microphone as her means of creative expression. After assembling her band, Patti knew at once they shared a guiding purpose. In *Just Kids*, she wrote:

> We imagined ourselves as the Sons of Liberty with a mission to preserve, protect, and project the revolutionary spirit of rock and roll . . .
>
> We would call forth in our minds the image of Paul Revere, riding through the American night, petitioning the people to wake up, to take up arms. We too would take up arms, the arms of our generation, the electric guitar and the microphone."

Artists Henri Matisse (1869-1954) and Pablo Picasso (1881-1973) are two fine examples of artists with a guiding purpose.

Matisse worked solidly for 50 years at his craft. Even after abdominal cancer and a difficult operation left the elderly artist bedridden, he continued to create works of art in the form of paper cut-outs until his death.

Matisse found a *joie de vivre* in his art that wasn't possible anywhere else, and he famously said, "Work cures everything."

Picasso, sensing his mortality, used his art to look death in the eye. The last of his works tackle subjects like human sexuality, physical decay and his looming death. He also left instructions for anyone in search of creative success.

 Our goals can only be reached through a vehicle of a

plan, in which we must fervently believe, and upon which we must vigorously act. There is no other route to success."

Both artists paid attention to what drove them. Each figured out the purpose of their lives and pursued it to the end.

The Personal Mission Statement

Admit it.

You're afraid of spending so much time alone with ideas that might never pay off when you could be earning real money and experiencing more success in a regular job. You're afraid of the disapproving looks from your friends and family when you go into your room or studio alone, again.

You're scared of wasting your time, of making the wrong decisions, of failing and, when you're honest with yourself, of not listening to the inner voice that whispers in the middle of the night, *create, damn it.*

Creative work involves so much ambiguity that you need a way of keeping motivated. You need a guiding purpose to navigate around your fears and explain, if only to yourself, why you do what you do.

No hard and fast rules ensure keeping motivated and figuring out what kind of creative person you are, but a personal mission statement will help.

A powerful support system, the personal mission statement will help you navigate the choppy currents of work and daily life.

When you face a big career decision, you'll be able to steer your craft in the right direction. You can use your mission statement to prevent being dashed upon the rocks or from getting stuck in shallow waters.

Now, you might be thinking a mission statement sounds like something a company or organisation would adopt, but in times of crisis or indecision, your personal mission statement will serve as your *oar.*

When I was unemployed, I used the exact process below to write my personal mission statement, find a way out of the darkness and decide what I was going to do with my career (or lack thereof).

Are you ready to get started?

Step 1: Map Your Life

Although you can do this at any time, a moment of crisis (like unemployment) is an ideal opportunity because you have the freedom to rethink every area of your life.

On a large piece of paper, map out the themes of your life and work down from there. Typically, these include relationships, career, health, finances, education, family and religion. Expand on each theme to include your commitments, responsibilities and any work you've accomplished so far.

Finished? Great.

Next, consider the roles you play in your life. These might include being a spouse, parent, employer/employee, student, brother/sister and so on. Expand on each of these roles in terms of your aims, beliefs, principles, progress to date and causes of concern.

It's not necessary to go into detail; the point is to capture only what's important in your life and what you've achieved so far, to pay attention to what drives you and to what keeps you up at 3:00 a.m.

Step 2: Draw on External Resources

Next gather quotes, information and lessons from books you read, talks you attended, places you visited, music or art that inspires you or people you met.

Consider what inspires you and gets you out of bed in the morning, what you crave and what you would keep doing even if you won the lotto.

Look at the creative role models in your professional or personal life and consider what you can learn from them.

Read their biographies and examine what drives those you

admire. See how they overcame personal and professional difficulties. Their lives should serve as a map that you can follow.

Spend time reading mission statements of others and see how they relate to your life. Undoubtedly your heroes took up many of the same roles and responsibilities that you now hold.

Journal writing is a great reflective practise for any creative professional, and if you keep one read through your older entries and look for a common theme or thread.

You should also consider organisations or people you *don't want to emulate* and determine how you can avoid making their mistakes. Remember, there's as much to learn from failure as from success.

Step 3: Ask Clarifying Questions

American mythologist and writer Joseph Campbell (1904-1987) famously told people to "follow your bliss" only to remark years later, that he should have said "Follow your blisters."

In other words, it's one thing to talk about following your passion, but you'll also need to take stock of what is causing you to struggle.

To do that, ask yourself searing questions about the themes of your life and each of your roles and areas of responsibility. Sample questions include:

- When am I at my best/worst as a parent/employer/employee/spouse/artist etc.?
- Where do my natural talents lie?
- What's important to me in my work/home life?
- What energises me, and what makes me feel apathetic?
- What is my passion?
- Who inspires me in my work, relationships, etc.?
- Which role models can I emulate?
- What values guide my work/my studies/my relationships?
- Are there core values or principles I am not prepared to violate (these can include charters that you join)?
- How do these values relate to my day-to-day life?

- What mistakes have I made in my life so far, and how I can avoid repeating them?

You can write these questions down in a journal or expand on them using a mind map. If you're less visually oriented, you could write a personal question and answer document. Use bullet points or just record your thoughts using pen and paper.

Step 4: Consider the Wider Canvas

In the trenches of daily life, most people don't have time to think about where and who they'd like to become over the next 12 months, five or even ten years.

Now that you know better, include a wish list of places to visit, creative projects to accomplish, and dreams to realise.

Consider what you could create if you had unlimited time, money and resources.

Identify projects in each area of your life that will help you accomplish these dreams. Your list might include things like releasing a best-selling album or publishing a popular thriller series.

Don't just think big. Think IMAX!

After you're done with grandiosity, consider how your future creative project will impact other important areas of your life. What kind of compromises might you need to make? What kind of obstacles will you have to overcome?

For example, you might need to go back to college to study music and improve your skills, the trade-off being to give up some financial resources and time away from your family.

Can you balance your creative goals with your personal values? Nobody is going to answer this question for you.

Finally, remember to consider what happens *after* you accomplish a major life goal. Will the sacrifices it costs to paint a masterpiece be worth it and what will you do next?

Irish singer and artist Glen Hansard (b. 1970) has dedicated his entire life to creating music, but after he won an Oscar for writing the song "Falling Slowly", he fell into a depression and drank heavily. He figured out how to live with success only after meeting Bruce Springsteen.

 He said that everything I had ever been in my life – that guy struggling against the world – had died the night we won the Oscar. I was in a different part of my life, a different suit. He said I should learn to embrace it, enjoy it."

Step 5: Bring It All Together

You're almost there.

Gather your information into a single document or source. Then, consolidate your roles, areas of responsibility, values, goals and dreams into several principles. Start with statements like:

- "I believe . . . "
- "I am happiest when . . . "
- "I stand by . . . "
- "I am at my best when . . . "

If you're stuck, write a few lines about what you'd like people to say about your life at your ninetieth birthday party or your funeral. The final result could be a mantra or motto that you repeat or a longer piece of work that you read or review regularly.

You could try a mind map, picture, logo or even a simple sentence like the photographer Robert Mapplethorpe (1946-1989) who wanted to "live for art."

There's no right or wrong approach. Instead, what you're looking to do is document a simple system of beliefs or personal rules to live by (and in turn create).

Step 6: Put Your Mission Statement Into Practise

Congratulations!

By now, you should have a working personal mission statement, but you're probably wondering, what should I do with it?

You could hang your mission statement on your wall or keep it somewhere private but accessible, or you could put it in your drawer. Alternatively, you could expand on your personal mission statement and develop one for your family.

Once you've created your mission statement, start setting goals for your creative projects and take action to achieve what you want.

Then, when you know what to do, go and do it because nothing disappoints more than an artist who knows what they want to achieve but never gets started.

When trouble arrives, as it inevitably will, you'll be self-reliant and have an oar to guide you through choppy waters.

Of course, all of this activity is useless without reflection. You don't want to spend years working on a creative project without occasionally asking yourself:

- "Is this worth doing?"
- "Am I living up to my personal beliefs?"
- "Do I know what's driving me?"

Put a few minutes aside once a month to review and update your mission statement and see if you're guiding your life in the right direction. You should have a system of personal beliefs that you refine as your life changes.

Work Beyond Chance and Fortune

You might be able to see the words in your head, have your colours arranged, a story at your fingertips or a muse for the camera, but you must act. Get the words out and your big ideas down.

Before you do, wait!

Pay attention to what's driving you. Decide what you want to achieve because, as the Stoic philosopher Lucius Seneca wrote, "When a man does not know what harbour he is making for, no wind is the right wind."

Now don't get me wrong, a personal mission statement is but one means of becoming unstuck and steering yourself towards the right harbour.

If it doesn't work for you, adopt a simple creed like the singer Patti Smith who lives for art or Pablo Picasso who had a creative plan he believed in until the very end.

A mission statement, a guiding purpose or even a simple artistic creed will help you sharpen your skills, develop your natural talents and spend your limited creative resources wisely.

Know that when you cast an oar into the river of life, you've already achieved more than those who are content to let chance and fortune carry them along.

My Personal Mission Statement

Below is my personal mission statement. When I showed this to a friend, he said he was impressed. I felt pleased with myself until he added, "You've a long way to go before you get there".

So take heart if yours feels ambitious. It doesn't have to look like mine. I've included mine as an example for you.

MY MISSION IS to pursue writing in all its forms and to create something from nothing. Writing is my shield and my sword, and this is how I will develop happiness.

I will teach my children how to become the kind of adults they were meant to be. I will demonstrate to them the virtues and challenges of temperance, love and patience. In doing so, I will foster these traits in myself.

I will seek physical and mental balance and avoid excess. I will avoid false and baseless pursuits and materialism because I know everything turns to ash. I will strive to reduce and refine rather than gather and accumulate.

I will practise empathy and conscientiousness. I will make sober decisions and embrace the idea of responsible risk-taking; that is I will live by Søren Kierkegaard's creed "To dare is to lose one's footing momentarily. Not to dare is to lose oneself."

I will lead a life of quiet integrity, for to speak ill of another is to damage myself. I will strive to understand the viewpoint of those I am against most. I will use moments of anger towards others as opportunities to learn more of my soul.

I will recognise my flaws, that I can become obsessive and impulsive, and I will seek to turn these flaws into virtues by becoming focused and brave. I will seek opportunities to practise kindness, temperance and patience because these are skills I must develop.

My time is finite. I will operate in my circle of influence rather than my circle of concern. I will put first things first. I will reflect upon the walls I am laying my ladders against.

I wither in stagnation, and I am energised when I am learning. I will burn myself completely like a good bonfire and leave no trace of myself behind (Shunryu Suzuki).

I will lean in.

Creative Takeaways

- Instead of letting life sweep you along, cast an oar into the river and guide yourself in the right direction.
- Do you have trouble making big decisions? Then, refer to your mission statement when you must make a decision as small as whether to practice when you don't feel like it or whether to invest in additional training.

4

LEARN WHAT YOUR CRAFT (AND YOUR AUDIENCE) DEMAND

"Begin challenging your assumptions. Your assumptions are the windows on the world. Scrub them off every once in awhile or the light won't come in."
– Alan Alda

I'M SITTING at a large wooden table with my notepad and pen in front of me, a steaming cup of coffee beside me. I'm inside a warm, heated log cabin miles from the nearest village. I have food, heating, a laptop, a stack of unread books and a bold idea.

It's almost 09:00 a.m., but I don't have to get up from my desk, walk out into the cold, strap myself in my car and sit in traffic for an hour before I reach work.

In the cabin, there's a comfortable bed, a stocked fridge, a large wooden table and pictures of Thomas Edison and the choreographer Twyla Tharp on the wall to inspire me.

I'm miles from the nearest shop. When I open my laptop, it doesn't ding or chime to notify me about emails, missed appointments and the demands of other people.

The mail carrier never calls. The phone doesn't ring. Here, alone in the woods, there is no one to keep happy, please or reassure.

I'm only interrupted when someone gently knocks on the door and leaves a breakfast of fresh fruit and strong coffee or a dinner of beef and Guinness stew sitting on the doorstep. I don't have to talk to anyone, thank anyone or apologise for what I'm doing.

Alone in the woods, I am finally free to work on my idea for hours at a time. I don't have to worry about what others think about me or my ideas.

And the problem with what I'm describing?

It's a fantasy.

Even if I could somehow find the time and resources to hole myself away in a creative retreat, there's little chance I'd finish something people would want to read in self-imposed solitude.

Would you?

Let me explain.

The idea of the lone artist toiling away in solitude, working on an idea for months or years at a time and then releasing a finished version of their work that succeeds is a falsehood.

I'm all for harnessing the power of solitude when you're at the start of a project, when you've no good ideas, when you want to practise your craft deliberately or become more comfortable with your work.

But, once you've given your idea form and substance you must expose it to the harsh light of critical, real-world feedback. You must test your underlying assumptions; see if your audience wants what you created. You must come out of the woods.

It's the only way to learn what your craft and your audience demand.

Pass the Salt

American businessman and inventor Thomas Edison (1847-1931) came up with thousands of inventions during his lifetime including the light bulb, a battery for an electric car and the motion picture camera.

A creative master, Edison challenged the assumptions of others – especially when he wanted to work with them.

When Edison met a potential employee, he tested the person's intelligence by asking a series of trivia questions like, "Where do we get prunes from?" or "Who invented printing?" and "What is felt?"

It was the early twentieth century after all.

Before offering a job, Edison took the applicant out for dinner and gave them a bowl of soup to eat. Then, Edison watched carefully to see what the job candidate did next.

If the unsuspecting candidate seasoned the soup with salt before tasting it, Edison didn't extend a job offer. On the other hand, if the candidate tasted the soup before seasoning it, Edison hired them.

He believed candidates who seasoned the soup without finding out if it needed salt was already full of unhelpful assumptions. This kind of person was of no use to Edison. He wanted to work with knowledgeable people who weren't full of preconceived ideas.

After all, this was a man who said, "Just because something doesn't do what you planned it to do doesn't mean it's useless."

Today, finding the origins of the prune is a Wikipedia search away. If you put the work in, read the right books and listen to the experts, you can school yourself on what you need to know about a topic or area of interest.

But the fundamentals of Edison's other test for job candidates remains: How can you challenge your assumptions?

Well, I'll be honest.

It's bloody hard to do it alone or if you're holed away in the woods.

I'd like to think if I reached Edison's shortlist, I'd sample his creamy vegetable soup before asking the waiter for the salt and pepper, but I'm an ordinary person with ordinary baggage and assumptions about how things should be.

I'd probably ask for the salt first.

Would you do the same?

Be honest.

If you're the kind of person who reaches for the metaphorical salt before tasting the soup, take a lesson from creative masters in the world of software development.

They are masters at challenging their assumptions, and they don't do it alone.

Learn What Your Audience Wants

Developing new software is an expensive and time-consuming business. The creative brains behind many of the tools and software programmes we use every day didn't get there by spending years of their lives and millions of dollars creating things people don't want.

Instead, many entrepreneurs turn their idea into a minimum viable product so they can challenge their assumptions and see if their customers want it *before* spending a significant amount of time or money on an idea.

Eric Reis (b. 1978) is an IT entrepreneur and author who popularised the concept of the minimum viable product. He explains:

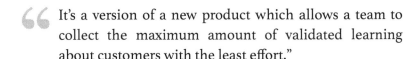 It's a version of a new product which allows a team to collect the maximum amount of validated learning about customers with the least effort."

Dropbox is an example of a successful minimum viable product.

Many great ideas are born because somebody had a problem they wanted to solve. Founder Drew Houston (b. 1983) came up with his idea for an easy-to-use file-sharing app because he was a forgetful MIT student.

He often left his USB behind, and every time he tried to share files with himself and others, he found technology was slow, buggy or difficult to use.

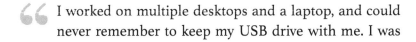 I worked on multiple desktops and a laptop, and could never remember to keep my USB drive with me. I was

drowning in email attachments trying to share files for my previous startup. My home desktop power supply literally exploded one day, killing one of my hard drives, and I had no backups."

Instead of reaching for the salt first and assuming his audience wanted his ideas, Houston developed an early concept. Then he created and narrated a three-minute video demonstrating the benefits of this easy-to-use file sharing service.

Houston packed his video with pop-culture Easter eggs and humorous references that resonated with the target audience of early adopters in the technology industry. At the end of the video, he asked viewers to register their interest by visiting the product's website.

Houston later said about his minimum viable product:

> It drove hundreds of thousands of people to the website. Our beta waiting list went from 5,000 people to 75,000 people literally overnight. It totally blew us away."

After watching the rapid growth of this waiting list, Houston knew his underlying assumptions were right. People wanted an easy-to-use file-sharing service that worked. And he had proof.

From there, Houston and his team avoided wasting time and resources on things like mainstream PR and developing features that beta users didn't want.

Instead, they built a simple product that worked and people wanted. Then they were able to acquire money and resources to turn their minimum viable product into something they could sell.

You might not be concerned with software or products, but nothing is more dispiriting than creating something no one wants. Wasting time, money and your creative energy hurts.

So, how can you find out what your audience wants instead of relying on assumptions?

Remember intuition is helpful, but knowing your idea works is better. So, get an early version or minimum viable product of your idea in front of your would-be audience or peers.

Ask them for constructive feedback that you can use to improve and expand upon your original idea.

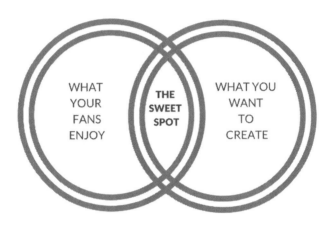

*Find the sweet spot between what you create and what your
fans will pay for*

IF YOU'RE A WRITER, release early chapters of your book to early or beta readers who provide you with feedback on how you can improve your work. Then, ask them if they'll pre-order your book so you have the financial resources to finish it.

Writer Hugh Howie (b. 1975), for example, didn't write all of his epic science-fiction series *Silo* in one go before releasing it. He wrote novella after novella and released each one separately because he recognised a demand for his ideas.

Others demonstrated their enthusiasm for his stories by opening their wallets.

If you're a musician, release some of your songs on social media or play them for people who aren't friends or family. Bands on tour often try out new and reworked songs in front of smaller audiences to see what works and what doesn't.

Bob Dylan (b. 1941) continually explores what his audience wants and likes. He constantly changes and rearranges his classic songs, sometimes to his audience's consternation and sometimes to their delight. He says,

 Getting an audience is hard. Sustaining an audience is hard. It demands a consistency of thought, of purpose, and of action over a long period of time."

If you're a painter, show an inner group of peers what you're working on, and use what they tell you to improve your work. Hell, even artists like Matisse and Picasso had patrons who supported their work financially *before* it was complete.

Your audience could love your idea; they could offer some harsh critical feedback or they could tell you it's terrible.

You could benefit from these opinions before you go any further. You don't want to spend months or years working on an idea only to find a big issue that's going to take months to fix or – worse – you've created something nobody wants.

After you've tested your minimum viable idea, you can do one of two things: Use your audience's critical feedback to improve your work or abandon your idea altogether and create something new.

Do you see what I'm saying? Good. Now that you know what your audience wants, let's cover . . .

Learn What Your Craft Demands

As a boy, Josh Waitzkin (b. 1976) was an American chess prodigy. He had an undeniable natural talent for the game, but what set him apart was how he learnt to play.

Waitzkin's coach Bruce Pandolfini presented Waitzkin with a barren chessboard and showed him how to play simple positions like king and pawn against a king. Once Waitzkin mastered these basic set pieces, Pandolfini added more pieces and built Waitzkin's knowledge incrementally. Waitzkin wrote:

> I was also gradually internalising a marvellous methodology of learning – the play between knowledge, intuition, and creativity. From both educational and technical perspectives, I learned from the foundation up."

Over the years and under the study of a few coaches, Waitzkin developed his knowledge of chess layer-by-layer, piece-by-piece and position-by-position. His peers, on the other hand, concentrated on learning complicated opening moves, assuming these short-term tactics would be enough to win any game.

> It's a little like developing the habit of stealing the test from your teacher's desk instead of learning to do the math. You may pass the test, but you learn absolutely nothing and most critically, you don't gain an appreciation for the value of learning itself."

As a competitor, Waitzkin faced a difficult problem. Loops from popular music songs, whispering spectators and the sound of a ticking clock kept getting stuck in his head while he was trying to concentrate. At first, this threw Waitzkin off his game, but he couldn't do anything about it.

He realised his craft demanded an ability to concentrate in an un-ideal environment. So, Waitzkin practised playing chess at home with music playing full-volume and gradually adjusted to the noise of a busy tournament.

Waitzkin went on to become a champion chess player, and he became an international master when he was 16.

Although he didn't have a minimum viable version of his ideas to test, this prodigy succeeded at chess partly because he used setbacks and victories as learning opportunities and to explore what his craft demanded.

Waitzkin is a creative master in more than chess. In his early twenties, he began studying the martial art Tai Chi Push.

To master this new art form, Waitzkin applied the same incremental approach to learning that he'd cultivated as a boy. It helped that years of competitive chess had already given him the mental discipline required to master a sport like Tai Chi.

Waitzkin rose quickly through the ranks of Tai Chi Push Hands and became a national champion in the United States.

In 2000, he competed in his first Push Hands World Championships in Taiwan. Waitzkin assumed the World Championships would be similar to the American competitions, but instead he found himself in an alien environment where no one spoke English or told him what was going on.

During the competition, the U.S. champion waited for his match for hours, getting hungry and anxious. Eventually, he ate a greasy pork lunch. Immediately afterwards, the announcer called his name to begin competing.

"I got destroyed," Waitzkin wrote about that match. "It wasn't even close."

After reflecting on his disappointing tournament, Waitzkin realised he wasn't prepared for the mental and physical demands of international competition.

Over the next few years, the former chess champion focused on his physical form and his mental attitude. He taught himself how to overcome setbacks like a last-minute change to the rules. Waitzkin even deliberately practised competing against a training partner, Frank, who didn't play by the rules.

Frank liked to jab his hand into Waitzkin's Adam's apple if he was about to lose a match.

"I quickly realised that the reason I got angry when he went after my neck was that I was scared," wrote Waitzkin. "There will always be creeps in the world, and I had to learn how to deal with them with a cool head."

Waitzkin competed again in 2002, and in 2004 he became a world champion title holder.

Although you might not be squaring off against a martial art competitor, your creative work still demands you learn new skills and hone existing ones like Waitzkin did.

Perhaps you need to teach yourself how to keep going when you feel like quitting. Or maybe learning to sit quietly in a room and paint or draw for two hours at a time without being distracted is your private victory.

Several years ago, I started tracking how long I spent writing, what I wrote and my daily word count in a spreadsheet. I'm not a numbers person, but this self-quantification helped me see exactly how much I was able to create each day and whether I was working as hard as I imagined.

I was able to compare my completed stories and articles against my word count for each month and discover when I was most and least creative. I also began writing down lessons about storytelling, writing, creativity and more so I could apply what I'd come across in my work.

Consider how you can track your creative output and start documenting lessons you've learnt about your craft in a journal or notebook.

If you're new, this kind of insight is invaluable because your peers, friends and family either won't understand or care about the strides you're making in your work.

They can see only the external output, the finished stories, the released music tracks, the photo collections and so on. Your audience has no way of measuring your growth as an artist or celebrating that you've learnt to deal with issues like fear and self-doubt.

In the end, you must mark these learning milestones, lest you forget them.

Create Alone and in Company

Learning what your craft or your audience demands is an art form.

When you're first acquiring a creative skill, start with the fundamentals. Although you won't have much to show for your hard work at first, build privately on each of your hard-earned lessons over time. Keep track of your progress so at least you can see how much you've come on and avoid reaching for the salt first.

As you become more accomplished at your chosen craft, don't give up on learning more of what your craft demands.

Like the meditator who discovers the intricacies of his or her breath by focusing on it each day, your work will reveal more to you over the weeks, months and years.

It's a lifelong practise, and it's one that separates the amateur from the professional and the professional from the creative master.

Consider what your audience wants too. When you're ready, show them a minimum viable idea and ask for critical feedback and if they're prepared to support you. Then, use their critical feedback or financial backing to improve your craft or ideas.

Of course, sometimes you don't need to worry about having a minimum viable idea.

If you're pursuing a passion project or a private creative work, by all means, do what you will. Or if your focus is an abstract project that you believe is pushing your chosen discipline forwards, then don't concern yourself with what others want.

History is full of instances when an inspired artist gave his or her audience something so shocking or original that they didn't know how to react. When Wolfgang Amadeus Mozart first released his music, his peers and audience lamented his composition was too rich in ideas, artful and difficult to understand.

Today, we could call these people Philistines but those moments are rare!

Remember, though, unless you've bought into the myth of the lone, starving artist, getting a minimum viable product or idea will help you test your assumptions and avoid wasting your limited time and creative energy.

The effort will help you learn more about your craft, faster.

So unless you're happy to create alone and in obscurity, trace the connection between what your audience wants and what you've created.

When you see a divide, bridge it.

Creative Takeaways

- Come out of your bat cave, go and meet your audience and show them what you've got. Study their reactions intensely.
- Start tracking your progress and what you've learnt about your craft.

5

FIND A CREATIVE MASTER

"No one is really going to help you or give you direction. In fact, the odds are against you."
– Robert Greene

STOP IT.

Stop feeling sorry for yourself.

You might think your problems are special, unique, or impossible for anyone else to understand. But you know what?

We're all struggling with the same basic creative problems.

You're not the only one who struggles, wants to think outside the box, needs motivation to keep going or craves critical feedback about their work.

You're not the only one who spends hours tinkering with your ideas and still hates them. And you're not the only one who'll do anything–clean the bathroom, service the car, run a marathon–to avoid sitting your ass in the chair and doing the work.

Almost every creative person faces problems like procrastination, perfectionism and self-doubt at one time or another. Even the successful ones.

But the feeling of being utterly alone on your artist's journey is insidious. It gnaws at your confidence and weakens your resolve. It causes talented writers to give up when all they need to do is keep going. And that needs to stop right now.

Your Map

Imagine the scene.

You're driving along a deserted road.

You haven't seen another car, another person or even a road sign in hours. The car's old engine has been making a strange rattling sound since you left home, and each time you hit another pothole, you think the engine might drop right out.

Regardless, you push your fears aside, sit up straight in your seat, and keep driving. Because while your destination is not on any map, others have told you it's worth the journey. But it'll be dark soon, and the fuel gauge is straying dangerously close to empty.

A while back, when my fuel gauge was close to empty, I came across advice from the recently departed American historical author E.L. Doctorow (1931-2015). He once said,

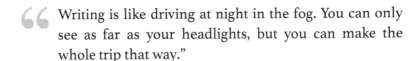 Writing is like driving at night in the fog. You can only see as far as your headlights, but you can make the whole trip that way."

It's a powerful metaphor and one you can apply to playing music, painting, drawing or most kinds of creative work. But if you're anything like me, you hate feeling lost.

You can't stand the sense that you might be on the wrong track, leaving a trail of wasted time and effort. Like anyone who works with ideas, I long for road markings or helpful directions from someone who has completed the same journey before me.

Seek Help from Past Masters

The mentor/student relationship is an age-old one.

By the thirteenth century, a young person in Western Europe who aspired to become a blacksmith, carpenter or even an artist served an apprenticeship. He or she worked for a master craftsman from age 15 onwards in exchange for food, board and instruction.

An apprenticeship lasted about seven years and, once complete, the young person could work as a journeyman or day labourer for wages.

Apprentices who aspired to become masters had to create a great work approved by the town guild and pay the group a hefty fee. As a master, they could take on apprentices and teach their skills.

Apprenticeships were expensive and sought after, and many of them never acquired a workshop of their own or became masters.

Today, having a mentor offers opportunities to learn a creative skill faster and gain access to the creative insight and resources of those who have gone before you.

Many modern-day creative masters sought the help of mentors to guide their careers.

For example, American writer Stephen King (b. 1947) attributes the success of his many books to his wife Tabby, who is also a writer. He shows Tabby early drafts of his books and asks her about tone, what he should put in and take out.

King counts on her as the one person who will say that he's working too hard or that he should slow down. It was Tabby who picked an earlier version of his first novel *Carrie* that agents rejected out from the wastepaper basket. She told a young and disillusioned King there was something in his story. He wrote,

 [Tabby] wanted me to go on with it . . . She wanted to know the rest of the story . . . 'You've got something here,' she said. 'I really think you do.'"

An ideal creative mentor takes more than a passing interest in

your work. These mentors want you to grow and develop as a creative person, and they will instruct you in their chosen art.

A mentor will show you how to avoid committing common mistakes and help you learn the skills of your creative trade faster. They will expose you to higher levels of creative thinking and provide you with critical feedback beyond what your friends, family, readers, listeners or critics offer.

You will become more accomplished and creative if you have a mentor to guide you, but *how can you find a mentor* and *what should you do once you've found one?*

Distinguish Between Good and Great Mentors

I spent my twenties trying and failing to earn a living as a successful Irish journalist. I would have given almost anything for a more experienced journalist to take an interest in the course of my career and show me what to do and what to avoid.

I was prepared to strike a Faustian pact, if you will.

Several of my classmates from journalism college worked with editors and more experienced colleagues who took an interest in their careers, but I always found it difficult to settle in a newspaper or radio station.

I grew resentful and was happy to tell people outside of the profession that most journalists were unhelpful.

I'd failed to see the big problem behind my petty resentments. During a career, people have many kinds of mentors. There are good mentors and great mentors; the former is easy to acquire while the latter is an elusive prize.

Good mentors are the teachers and instructors in your local creative writing, music or film class. They are respected colleagues in the workplace or even some of your friends.

Even more importantly, they can help you advance your creative career faster, even if you work with or follow that mentor for just a little while.

The good news is it's relatively easy to find a good mentor. A more experienced colleague that you can trust can serve this role for a time (although you might not want to label the relationship) or you can hire a teacher or instructor to work directly with you.

Great mentors are fewer and farther between and harder to find. They are creative masters whose work keeps you up at night because it's so damn good.

So how can you find a great mentor?

If that person is still living and working, figure out how you could be useful to them. Try to look at the world through the gaze of your mentor, asking yourself, "What does he or she need most?"

Transform yourself into someone with skills that complement their work.

Yes, this means you're going to have to work for free. I know giving away your time for nothing is troubling, but I'd like to reframe what you're doing as a trade: Your time for access to their expertise.

Great mentors almost always complain about a lack of free time. One great way to hook their attention is to do something that gives your would-be mentor more hours to spend. If you're a writer, for example, you could offer to write an article or a blog post for their website.

You can also work with great mentors as part of a group.

Let's say you are a musician.

You and several of your peers could sign up for a workshop or retreat with a talented musician during which your mentor provides you and the rest of the group critical feedback over a couple of days.

You can also short-circuit this process if you're prepared to either pay a great mentor for one-on-one feedback or if you shift your definition of the student/mentor relationship.

Your Council of Mentors

What I'm going to tell you next makes me sound crazy.

I talk to dead people.

No, I'm not referring to ghosts or strangers who haunt my house. I

talk to American novelist and short story writer John Cheever
(1912-1982).

Known as the "Chekhov of the suburbs," he wrote five novels and
a number of short story collections during his creative career. Six
weeks before his death, Cheever was awarded the National Medal for
Literature by the American Academy of Arts and Letters.

He died in 1982 when I was only a year old.

So if I never met Cheever and he died when I was a baby, how can
he be one of my creative mentors?

Several years ago, I read *The Journals of John Cheever*, a book that
gave me insight into his creative process. Then I read several of
Cheever's novels, as well as books by writers who influenced him.

Tracing the roots of his big ideas helped me understand why
Cheever made some of his creative choices and gave me more of a
feeling for what inspired him as a writer.

For a long time afterwards, when faced with a creative challenge I
visualised Cheever and asked him, "What would you do?" Now, his
manifesto guides me.

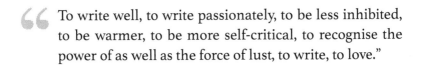 To write well, to write passionately, to be less inhibited,
to be warmer, to be more self-critical, to recognise the
power of as well as the force of lust, to write, to love."

I'm aware this makes me sound quite mad, but it's a creative
process that American author Napoleon Hill (1883-1970) recommended in his seminal book *Think and Grow Rich!*

He suggested keeping an "imaginary council" every night that
you consult when you have a problem or need advice.

He wrote,

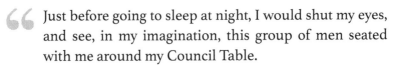 Just before going to sleep at night, I would shut my eyes,
and see, in my imagination, this group of men seated
with me around my Council Table.

I had a very definite purpose in indulging my
imagination through these nightly meetings. My

purpose was to rebuild my own character so it would represent a composite of the characters of my imaginary counsellors."

Hill's council comprised nine of his mentors including Thomas Edison and Charles Darwin–people Hill never met. There's no psychological trickery behind his approach either.

Instead, push yourself to learn from every possible source that your imaginary mentor offers. Read the books they cite, listen to what inspired them and trace the roots of their creative work until you unearth their influences. Be rigorous about applying what your mentor has to teach.

Be Selective

What if you're working with a mentor who got lucky or one who doesn't know what they are doing? What if their teachings are stale and out of date? What if your values clash with theirs?

Before you select your creative mentor, research your needs and their qualities thoroughly.

To find out if a creative mentor is suitable, write a list of your weaknesses, needs and areas where you need improvement.

Perhaps you need help playing musical scales, adding texture to your paintings or weaving stories into your works. Or maybe you're struggling to learn from each of your practise sessions. Or perhaps you need help with the tactics of your craft. And so on.

Find a mentor who is farther along the path you're walking or turn towards a mentor who has mastered one of your obvious deficiencies. They must be able to help you address the areas where you need help.

Read everything about your potential mentor and find critics of their work so you can assess whether the relationship will work. It's best to discover the potential flaws of your would-be mentor before you've invested a significant amount of time, money and creative resources following their path.

Once you spend money or time on a mentor, this sunken cost complicates turning away from their teachings, even if it's foolish to throw good money after bad.

When you are selecting a mentor, consider your psychology.

Ask honest questions about your tolerance for risk and failure.

Many creative masters take bold and dramatic risks on the path towards success and fail hard before they achieve their goals.

Stephen King's novel *Carrie* was rejected 30 times before his wife fished it out of the bin. Walt Disney was a creative visionary, but he spent much of his career teetering on the brink of bankruptcy and even voiced contempt for the financial backers who helped him out.

J.K. Rowling wrote the first Harry Potter book while jobless, divorced and raising a child alone.

Do you have the stomach for these kinds of risks and failures?

A great mentor doesn't have to become your friend, but you must be able to listen to them without feeling irritated or despondent. Consider how you will react to their beliefs, leadership style, way of thinking, systems, mannerisms, speech and ideals.

Remember, a great mentor will help you connect ideas in exciting ways, think on a higher level and achieve your creative goals faster. Choose well!

Burn Your Mentor's Ideas Into Your Own

Read, watch and listen to everything your mentor sends you, produces or creates. Keep a file or a notebook and write down every-thing they have to teach you and review regularly what you've learnt from them.

Whenever you face a decision about how to spend your time or resources, use your mentor's teachings to guide you. Ask them ques-tions and, if possible get them to review your work and provide crit-ical feedback.

Do what they tell you, and put as much of their teachings into practise as you can at the expense of advice you hear elsewhere. The fire of your mentor's teachings should temper you so that you can face external ideas and challenges without becoming over-whelmed.

At first, your mentor's advice might seem odd and even against your better instincts, but remember your mentor knows far more about the creative journey you're both on.

Later, when you start to achieve results, you can bring more of your experiences and knowledge into your chosen creative field.

Nothing lasts forever.

There will come a point when you must develop self-reliance and strike out on your own. It will naturally arrive if you've hired a mentor to work with you for a pre-determined period or if they're working with you in a more distanced capacity. Be sure you're both prepared to make the break.

If you are working directly with your mentor and have hooked their attention, they might become dependent on you and even hold you back.

They might want to keep you within the fold because they need you or even because they are afraid you will outshine them.

If this happens, remember the goal of any mentoring relationship isn't life-long friendship; your creative work must come first.

Prepare for the Journey Ahead

The road at the beginning of any creative journey appears long and mysterious. Realising you've got only a vague idea of where you're going or wondering if you're going to reach your destination soon is never pleasant.

Yes, the look of *your* journey will be different from the next person's, but make no mistake: You are not the first person to embark on this creative path.

Many others are willing to show you the way if you have the guts to ask. Follow the path that writers, artists, painters, filmmakers and creative masters have walked before you. The next time you encounter a creative problem, ask yourself what would your mentor do.

As you become more skilled at your craft, start questioning some of your mentor's ideas and teachings.

Challenge your mentor.

They might not like this pushback, and many mentor/student relationships end acrimoniously. However, if you go into this type of relationship with your eyes open, you will be prepared for the inevitable end of the mentor/student relationship.

When you reach this crossroad, look for another, better mentor to guide you.

Say to yourself: *Onwards!*

You can draw on the strengths of one mentor to offset the weaknesses of the next. It's why writers work with more than one editor during their career, and it's why musicians move from one producer to the next.

By tapping into the knowledge of multiple experts, you will fashion yourself into a creative person other people seek out.

By going from one creative mentor to the next, you will combine the teachings of various teachers with your unique ideas and creative voice.

This combination of the accomplished and the new will help you grow into an exciting and fresh creative talent.

You just have to be brave enough to keep going.

Creative Takeaways

- Write down a hit list of people you would like to have as your creative mentor. Remember, they can be alive, dead, accessible or inaccessible.
- Next time you face a creative challenge, visualise your mentor and ask what would they do.

6

STRENGTHEN YOUR MIND AND YOUR BODY

"Pain is inevitable. Suffering is optional."
– Haruki Murakami

"THINGS AREN'T GOING WELL for you here Bryan," my boss said.

I was working as a press officer for a charity. It was supposed to be my dream job. You know the kind: Earn an honest wage, work nine-to-five hours, drink nice coffee and tell myself I'm finally making a difference in the world.

I was all for it, and this was my first performance review.

"Are you listening, Bryan?" my boss asked. "You missed an important deadline; you caused confusion for other members of your team, and there were mistakes in your work."

On a Wednesday morning in November, we were sitting in a quiet room away from the hum of the office.

"There's so much to learn," I said.

I accepted I was guilty of mistakes, of incompetence. I produced an important report with typos, a presentation with incorrect slides and I'd missed a meeting with a client.

"I'm sorry. I can do better, just give me more time."

He adjusted narrow-frame silver glasses. "You've got three months, but you need to put that master's you studied for into action."

"I'll try," I said. "I'll do better."

That night, I bought a popular book about productivity and implemented every strategy I could understand. I reread my boss's emails, searching for actions I'd missed.

I sent the management team weekly updates of my accomplishments. I even pinned a quote from Viktor E. Frankl's *Man's Search For Meaning* to the wall near my desk.

> Live as if you were living already for the second time and as if you had acted the first time as wrongly as you are about to act now."

I embraced the job, but no matter what I did I couldn't figure out how to give my boss (and his boss) what they needed. Every project I worked on failed. I tried to send e-Christmas cards to the charity's mailing list only to find I'd compiled a list of the wrong recipients.

I created a development plan for the charity's website that my boss didn't want to read, and I wrote a 2,000-word profile of the organisation's work that the management team said they couldn't publish.

I felt as if I were under attack.

After Christmas, my boss called me back into that room.

"We're letting you go, Bryan. The work you're doing here isn't much beyond that of a clerical officer in the civil service, and that's not what this charity needs." My boss slid a white envelope across the table. "Here's your notice."

I felt like taking the envelope, ripping it up and throwing it at him. Not even Viktor Frankl could help me.

"I left a good job to come here." I thought of the permanent and pensionable job I'd had as care worker for people with intellectual disabilities.

"What am I supposed to do now?" I asked.

"This is hard for me," he said. "I know it must be hard for you."

I folded the envelope in two.

How could this be hard for him when I was the one losing a job in the middle of a recession with my wife and two small children depending on me?

"When do I finish?"

He folded his hands.

"We'll give you till the end of February alongside whatever holiday pay you're due."

I left the room and walked out the front door and into the small car park. I got into my rusting 2002 Renault Clio. Then I punched the ceiling over and over and swore as loudly as I could get away with in a business park at 3:00 p.m. on a grey Monday afternoon in January.

For weeks afterwards, I was angry about being fired, being out of a job and claiming social welfare. I tried to write about it, but I didn't make much progress.

I couldn't find a way to balance my anger and disappointment with the calmness writing demands. and the endurance I needed to look for another job.

I looked outwards toward the biographies of artists I admired for answers. I wanted to see how they overcame personal and professional setbacks and still found strength to work on their ideas.

What I found surprised me. Some of these creative masters lived deeply unhappy lives, while others knew how to change their destructive habits for the better.

The Drunken Miserable Artist

Do you believe alcohol or drugs unlocks fresh thinking that sobriety can't? Are you prepared to sacrifice present or future happiness for more inspired ways of thinking?

A pernicious myth suggests the best artists are unapologetic drug addicts and alcoholics. They take pride in being tortured souls who tap into a higher creative power. They can only support their immense talents with the crutch of alcohol and drugs.

Yes, alcohol and drugs will help you view the world differently and even come up with original ideas . . . at least at first.

Neuroscientist and philosopher Sam Harris (b. 1967) consumed psychedelic drugs such as LSD and magic mushrooms in his early twenties as part of his search for new ideas about the universe and himself. However, Harris likens his approach to strapping himself to a rocket ship.

> If LSD is like being strapped to a rocket, learning to meditate is like gently raising a sail. Yes, it is possible, even with guidance, to wind up someplace terrifying, and some people probably shouldn't spend long periods in intensive practise. But the general effect of meditation training is of settling ever more fully into one's own skin and suffering less there."

Artists like William Faulkner, Ernest Hemingway, John Cheever, Raymond Carver, F. Scott Fitzgerald, Amy Winehouse, Vincent Van Gogh, Yoko Ono, John Berryman and Neil Young were compelled to strap themselves to their personal rocket ships, but look closer and you'll see that these artists also recognised the value of sobriety.

Take Ernest Hemingway (1899-1961). He was a prolific and inspired writer, but he was also notorious for drinking heavily. His biographer Anthony Burgess wrote:

> The manager of the Gritti Palace in Venice tells me . . . that three bottles of Valpolicella first thing in the day were nothing to him, then there were the daiquiris, Scotch, tequila, bourbon, vermouthless martinis. The physical punishment he took from alcohol was . . . actively courted."

Although he struggled with alcoholism, Hemingway went to great lengths to sober up before the end his life, and he never wrote while drunk. In *Interview Magazine*, Hemingway's granddaughter, Mariel, said about him,

> That's not how he wrote. He never wrote drunk, he never wrote beyond early, early morning . . . So many writers glorify my grandfather's way of living as much as they glorify his work. And so they try and mirror that. I think it's the misperception of addiction and living life on the edge, as if it's cool."

Hemingway struggled until the very end.

On Saturday the 2nd of July 1961, Hemingway rose early, unlocked the storage room of his house in Ketchum, Idaho, and took out a shotgun he used for shooting pigeons. Hemingway walked to the foyer of his house, put the twin barrels against this forehead, and pressed the trigger.

The American poet John Berryman (1914-72) relied on drink to stabilise him and offset the startling intensity he brought to his poetry. He got into drunken arguments with his landlord, was arrested, fell, suffered hallucinations, was hospitalised, gave public lectures that he couldn't remember and was divorced three times.

While in treatment in 1970, he wrote,

"Wet bed drunk in a London hotel, manager furious, had to pay for a new mattress, $100. Lectured too weak to stand, had to sit. Lectured badly prepared. Too ill to give an examination, colleague gave it. Too ill to lecture one day. Literary work stalled for months. Quart of whiskey a day for months. Wife desperate, threatened to leave unless I stopped. Two doctors drove me to Hazelden last November, 1 week intensive care unit, 5 wks treatment. AA 3 times, bored, made no friends. First drink at Newlbars' party. Two months light drinking, hard biographical work. Suddenly began new poems 9 weeks ago, heavier & heavier drinking more & more, up to a quart a day. Defecated uncontrollably in university corridor, got home unnoticed.

Book finished in outburst of five weeks, most intense work in my whole life exc. maybe first two weeks of 1953."

While reading that, my heart went out to Berryman's suffering, to a man who never found an answer to his problems. On Friday, January 7, 1972, he got the bus to Washington Avenue Bridge, climbed onto the railing, fell 100 feet, missed the Mississippi River and landed on a nearby embankment.

Short story writer and poet Raymond Carver (1938-1988) struggled with alcohol for years, too.

In late 1977, he went to a dinner party with friends, drank a glass of wine and blacked out. The next thing he remembered was standing outside a store the following morning waiting for it to open so he could buy a bottle of vodka. Then he attended a meeting with an editor who wanted to buy his book; Carver was both drunk and hungover.

It was enough of a low for Carver to finally find a better way to live with his pain. He told the *Paris Review* about his decision to quit drinking,

 I stayed drunk for a couple more days. And then I woke up, feeling terrible, but I didn't drink anything that morning. Nothing alcoholic, I mean. I felt terrible physically--mentally, too, of course--but I didn't drink anything. I didn't drink for three days, and when the third day had passed, I began to feel some better. Then I just kept not drinking. Gradually I began to put a little distance between myself and the booze. A week. Two weeks. Suddenly it was a month. I'd been sober for a month, and I was slowly starting to get well."

After he stopped drinking, Carver enjoyed 10 good and creative years before dying of cancer at age 50. In the poem "Gravy" – which is inscribed on his grave – he wrote:

"Don't weep for me,"
he said to his friends. "I'm a lucky man.
I've had ten years longer than I or anyone
expected. Pure Gravy. And don't forget it."

Ten years doesn't seem like much, but Carver used these years to give his creative work the respect and attention it demanded, and unlike some of his peers, he found a measure of happiness.

The stories of these creative masters demonstrates that creativity demands clear, level-headedness, and that pure gravy will come only if you're healthy and strong.

The Unbreakable Link Between Mind and Body

So, you want to become the kind of artist who has the energy to turn up every day in front of the blank page and create. You're looking for a way of focusing on your big idea without getting distracted, and you'd like to finish what you're working on without sacrificing your happiness.

If only there were something that would help you do all this . . . without strapping yourself to a rocket ship.

There is.

For me, the best, most creative days come when I run and meditate. Meditation and exercise will help you embrace positive change in many different ways. Many productive artists pursue activities like these.

I've spent some tough times here.

Focus on Your Big Ideas

Meditation is scientifically proven to aid concentration, improve our memory and make us smarter. Those who meditate for 20 or more minutes thrice a week are better able to focus on a task and less prone to mood swings.

Running is a lot like meditation.

Think about it:

Both meditation and running demand that you turn up several times a week on your cushion or in your trainers and commit to one difficult task for an extended period.

Both activities involve focusing on the breath at length, just as aspiring artists must learn to concentrate on the ideas before them.

The runner knows one bad training session doesn't mean they are unfit or unprepared for a race. The next day, they simply put their trainers back on and keep going.

The meditator acknowledges day-to-day setbacks alongside small accomplishments, accepting both as they move forward.

If you're an artist who exercises intensely (or meditates), a short story, painting or a complicated piece can feel more achievable. You can take the lessons learnt on the track or the cushion and break down a big idea into a series of small milestones.

Then you can focus on achieving small personal victories, overcoming minor setbacks and slowly progressing towards your goal.

Give Your Monkey Mind a Break

If you're a desk monkey like me, you spend up to eight hours a day looking at a screen, in your office on your phone, and in front of the television.

Like me, you might look at your bloodshot eyes in the mirror and wonder if all this screen time is rotting your brain, killing your concentration and making you go blind.

Your body and mind crave a break from the glare of screens, monitors and devices.

Give them what they want.

Then when you sit down to work on your creative project, you will be able to see the hook for your article, the typo on page two and the plot twist that your tired, overworked mind missed an hour ago.

Transform into a More Productive Artist

As a writer, I'm fascinated by how artists get things done. Here's what I discovered:

Most creative masters are nothing like Ernest Hemingway or John Berryman. They aren't alcoholics; they are disciplined, sober and health-conscious. Also, Hemingway and Berryman both tried to sober up towards the end.

Take Haruki Murakami (b. 1949). He is one of Japan's greatest novelists and the author of books like *Kafka on the Shore* and *What I Talk About When I Talk About Running*. He's also a serious athlete who runs at least one marathon a year. When Murakami is writing a novel, he says he runs or swims for at least an hour a day.

 Exerting yourself to the fullest within your individual limits: That's the essence of running, and a metaphor for life – and for me, for writing as well. I believe many runners would agree."

When I'm in pain, I think of that sentence. I force myself to run a little farther, a little harder. Later, I try to write a while longer and go that bit deeper.

Fight Depression and Eliminate Stress

Steven Pressfield wrote in *Turning Pro* when the professional artist is in pain, he or she takes "two aspirin and keeps on trucking", but even he would agree it's easier to work on your ideas when you're not in pain.

The good news is intense physical exercise like running helps you lose weight, fight disease and sleep better, and when you are physically and mentally healthier, you are better able to concentrate on your ideas.

If good health isn't enough reason to run, anyone who trains several times a week experiences a runner's high, which I can vouch for. The natural feel-good endorphins that running releases carry over after you've finished, into your work.

When I run five or ten kilometres, the chair, my computer, the keyboard, the blank screen, and the flashing cursor all become irresistible.

You might be thinking,

Stop, I hate running!

Swap running for any aerobic activity, and you'll get all the benefits listed above.

You can swim, cycle, box, golf, row, ski, dance, play tennis or squash, hike or even cut grass, and still become a more productive and creative writer.

Letting Go

I discovered meditation before being fired.

I first considered it a way to focus on work and become a model employee. But then I found myself without a job, and the intimidating red cushion demanded, "Sit!".

I refused to sit for weeks.

To sit and look inwards, to face my anxiety and disappointment when I should have been working and writing struck me as preposterous.

Damn that cushion!

One day I received a rejection for a new job I was perfect for. I brooded about it all day, and I argued with my wife about money that evening. Later that night, I tossed and turned in bed and considered who had wronged me.

At 3:00 a.m., I got up, went downstairs and sat on the large red cushion. I clasped my hands, took a deep breath and closed my eyes. I meditated on the faces of my family and thanked them for their support. I meditated on the faces of people I worked with, and I wished them well in their careers.

Finally, I meditated on the face of my boss. I could see his pale, lined face, his crisp white shirt and his dark wavy hair. My hands tightened, my foot began to ache, and a line of sweat ran down the small of my back.

"I forgive you for letting me go," I said.

I won't lie. Ten minutes of meditation didn't siphon all my anger, but it pierced a hole, and enough eased out that I could sleep.

Finding meaningful employment took another six months.

Several weeks into a new role in a profession I didn't expect, I thought of my old boss and the pressure he was under from his boss. In my journal, I wrote about how he didn't have to give me holiday pay or write me a good reference and of how he did all of those things.

Through the one thing I knew how to do before I was fired and the one thing I kept trying to do after I was fired – writing – I saw my mistakes for what they were and the role for what it was: One I wasn't built for. And it was OK.

I could learn to let go too.

Creative Takeaways

- Cultivate physical and mental strength and endurance so you can approach the blank page or virgin canvas without fear.
- Your pursuit of physical and mental strength and endurance should support your creative work, not the other way around.

7

INVEST IN YOUR SIDE PROJECTS

*"A musician must make music, an artist must paint, a poet must write, if he
is to be ultimately at peace with himself."*
– Abraham Maslow

AFTER WRITING a lengthy charity grant application for several weeks, I
was exhausted. When my boss at my main gig asked me to perform
simple tasks, I tried not to snap at her.

When my friends asked how the new job was going and if I was
still writing, I cracked cynical jokes about how it was a waste of time.

I didn't know it then, but I was burnt-out and unhappy.

Christina Maslach from The University of California Berkeley
and Susan E. Jackson from NYU are authorities on this subject.

They said workers who are burnt-out "feel unhappy about themselves and dissatisfied with their accomplishments on the job."

I blame myself.

I should have listened to Abraham Maslow.

In 1943, this American psychologist explained individuals can be
happy only if they can express themselves and achieve their potential. These were all things I wasn't doing.

If you're a musician, you must play, if you're a writer, you must get the words down, and if you're an artist, you must fill the virgin canvas.

Maslow called this "self-actualisation" and cautioned "the story of the human race is the story of men and women selling themselves short."

Don't sell yourself short.

If your main gig isn't giving you enough time or space to write, draw, paint or play, if you spend your nine-to-five responding to the demands of others, or if you work on projects only because they pay the bills, you need a side project.

Hell, even if you love your main gig, a side project will prevent you from becoming burnt-out, and it could put food on your table down the road.

Recognising Side Projects

When you're messing around and jamming, when it's just for kicks, when nobody gets hurt, gets paid or gets laid, it's a side project.

When you're working alone with an idea and an editor isn't screaming about deadlines, it's a side project.

When it's an idea for a TV show you carry on set every day and pull out when you've got a few free hours, it's a side project.

When it's a band you play with for fun after your main gig is done, it's a side project.

When you take pictures for hours at the weekend and stay up late at night fretting about white balance and colour compositions, it's a side project.

When it's a haiku you write on the back of a white envelope in between boardroom meetings, it's a side project.

When you're bored and sitting on the train or waiting for a plane and you're doodling on the back of a beermat, it's a side project.

When you can't bring yourself to throw it away, it's a side project.

When you're stuck, blocked and procrastinating, when your main thing is the painful thing, it's a side project.

When you think you're messing around, and something unexpected happens, it's a side project.

When you knock your big ideas off each other like billiard balls, it's a side project.

When they produce an unexpected little idea, it's a side project.

When it's the fun you have when all the other work is done, it's your side project.

Just ask Matthew Weiner.

How Matthew Weiner Carved Out Time for His Side Project

Ever since he was a boy, Matthew Weiner (b. 1965) wanted to become a writer. He was born into a home in Baltimore that revered writers, but when Weiner attempted to follow in the footsteps of his creative heroes, he was rejected time and again.

He wrote poetry and stories and tried to join writing class after writing class. A professor who read some of Weiner's early poetry told him, "I think you know you are not a poet."

Weiner studied literature, philosophy and history at Wesleyan University and attended film school at the University of Southern California.

After graduating, he stayed at home for three years and spent his time writing spec scripts for television shows.

While his friends got real, paying day jobs, Weiner struggled to break into show business as a writer. He relied on his wife, who was an architect, to support him.

Like many new artists, Weiner couldn't handle the constant rejection and lack of success. His main gig wasn't paying off. So he stopped writing and considered getting a real job that paid well with the rest of his friends.

Then, Weiner got a break that changed his life.

Through an old college friend, Weiner found his first paying job as a television writer for a pilot that needed a polish or a "punch-up".

Weiner's new main gig involved working fourteen hour days, but his obvious writing talents impressed the writers and producers, and they used some of Weiner's suggestions in the pilot.

After getting his first paying job as a writer, Weiner went on to write for popular comedies like *Becker*. When Weiner wasn't working on his main gig, he spent his free time in the mornings and at night working on a side project.

This time, he didn't expect it to pay the bills. He had an idea for a little television show about the lives of a group of successful but unhappy advertising executives during the 1950s and 60s.

In the book *Getting There*, he tells Gillian Zoe Segal about this side project:

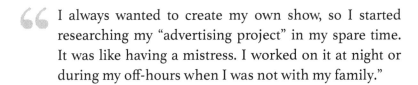 I always wanted to create my own show, so I started researching my "advertising project" in my spare time. It was like having a mistress. I worked on it at night or during my off-hours when I was not with my family."

Weiner faced a new problem. Putting in 14-hour days at the main gig didn't leave him enough free time or energy to get the words down on the page at night. Weiner could have put his big idea on the shelf, but like a lot of creative masters, he didn't quit.

Instead, Weiner used earnings from his main gig to hire a transcriber to record his ideas. He also hired a researcher to help him unearth small details that gave his side project more authenticity. Weiner says:

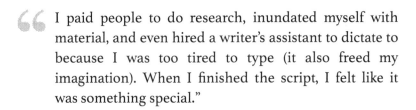 I paid people to do research, inundated myself with material, and even hired a writer's assistant to dictate to because I was too tired to type (it also freed my imagination). When I finished the script, I felt like it was something special."

When Weiner wasn't working on his main thing, he lived with his side project. He carried a script for *Mad Men* everywhere he went. He showed it to his colleagues and David Chase, the director, creator and writer of *The Sopranos*.

Chase was so impressed by the script that he hired Weiner as a writer and supervising producer. He said about Weiner's idea,

> It was lively, and it had something new to say . . . Here was someone who had written a story about advertising in the 1960s, and was looking at recent American history through that prism."

At first, while working on *The Sopranos*, Weiner put his script aside for the most part. Later when *The Sopranos* drew to an end, Weiner pitched his big idea to producers on the side.

Before the final season of *The Sopranos* aired, Weiner sold *Mad Men* to the ABC television network because, "They were trying to make a splash and wanted to do something new."

Finally realising his dream, Weiner became show runner for *Mad Men* and filmed 13 episodes of season one. What started out as a side project became a hit TV show that ran for seven seasons and won 16 Emmys as well as four Golden Globes.

The Unexpected Origin of this Book

I started writing this book as a side project. I've always wanted to learn about creativity and to find out how great writers, musicians, artists, filmmakers and creative masters find and deliver their big ideas.

I spent two years reading articles and books about the lives and working habits of creative people like Albert Einstein, Leonardo da Vinci and more modern creative masters like Steve Jobs, Twyla Tharp and Matthew Weiner.

I didn't set out to write a book about creativity, but the more I read about these people, the more I used what I learnt as fuel for my writing projects.

I also kept everything I discovered in a file on my computer and without knowing it I began to assemble the spine of a book piece by piece.

While gathering this information, I continued working on my main gig, which included finishing a collection of short stories, finishing a book about productivity and working full-time.

In the summer of 2015, I reviewed the information and research. I gathered it in one place and realised I'd accumulated enough for a book about creativity. The sheer volume of information suggested to me I had an idea to complete.

I faced a choice. I could have continued writing fiction in my free time or I could turn my unearthed ideas and research into a nonfiction book about creativity.

I decided to turn a little side project that had been bubbling away at the back of my mind into a big one. So I began to organise my ideas and research relevant themes, and I took time out from whatever else I was working on to write this book.

I share this humble origin so you can see side projects are an important pursuit for anyone who wants to become more creative.

Now let's explore how you can get more from your creative side projects:

Switch to Your Side Project When You Need a Break

I love creative side projects because they help me procrastinate and still get things done. They help me avoid feeling like I want to pull my hair out when I'm working at my main gig.

They also help me cultivate new creative habits without taking massive risks or investing a lot of time and money into a single idea.

The next time you're struggling with your main gig and think, "Oh God, I just don't have the energy, the passion or any good ideas to face into this today," pick up your side project and work on that instead.

Do it for five minutes, do it for an hour, or do it for an entire day. Then return to your main gig with the energy of someone who's just back from a refreshing holiday in the sun.

If you're lucky enough to love your main gig, switching gives you a much-needed break from a troublesome idea and enables you to practise your creative skills in a different way. You could even be nudging your career along like Weiner did.

Experiment Without Expectation

Consider your side project a creative experiment that will give you a new perspective on your craft. Defer critical decisions like a final deadline or the ending of a story.

You've got a chance to become tolerant of the ambiguity that comes with not having reached a decision or closed a loop; so seize it!

Practise accepting the discomfort of having an open loop, an unreached decision or a final cut: all luxuries you probably don't have while at your main gig. Use your side projects to practise facing your fears.

Avoid pressing hard for a great idea or for something you must use. You're free to abandon reason, logic and even clarity. Be reckless and bold with your ideas.

If you fail or if the experiment blows up in your face, this isn't a catastrophe because you haven't invested all of your emotional, financial or creative resources in your side project.

Break It Down

You shouldn't feel intimidated by the scale and ambition of your side project.

If you do, break your side project down into little treats you enjoy or that offer a relief when your main gig is turning sour.

Today, it's enough to read up on the background for your television script. Tomorrow, it's sufficient to transcribe your notes. It's enough because there are no expectations. It's only you and your ideas.

Here's a caveat:

You must progress your side project in some small way and not just hold it in the back of your mind or talk about it with friends over a beer.

Matthew Weiner would never have filmed *Mad Men* if all he did was tell his friends he had a great idea for a television show and that he'll get around to working on it someday.

Don't Quit Your Day Job (Yet)

Do you have bills, small kids or a spouse to provide for? If you quit your job because you want to spend all day alone with your side project, expect to hear from your bank manager.

Here's the thing:

Your main gig is giving you a fantastic opportunity to play with a side project early in the morning or late at night. Even if it doesn't fire you up, it's keeping the lights on at home.

You have freedom and licence to work on your side project without fear of failure because your main gig is taking care of business.

But what if you can afford to quit the day job and work on your side project all day?

Once you do this, your side project becomes your new job.

You'll have to finish it, ensure it pays the bills and keeps the lights on. You won't be free to take as many creative risks or experiment, and there will be things about your side project that you won't enjoy, but you'll have to do them if you want to feed your family.

While You're There, Work Hard at It

Would Matthew Weiner have become a successful television writer for *The Sopranos* (thus earning the respect and mentorship of David Chase) if he had obsessed about *Mad Men* on set and paid no attention to the television show he was being paid to create?

Probably not.

When you're at your main gig, devote yourself to it.

Then, consider how you can use the skills and resources you're acquiring during the nine-to-five to advance your side project in some small way.

Perhaps you're a marketer, and you can use what you learn on the job to sell more of your art?

Perhaps, like Weiner you're a television writer, and you can use your connections to pitch your ideas to other producers.

Maybe you're a web designer, and you're able to use your design skills to create a website for your side project.

Even if your main gig has nothing to do with your side project or your art, use what they pay you (after the bills are taken care of) to hire an editor, designer, producer or mentor and buy the materials you need for your side project.

Combining Your Experiences

Work on different things at the same time, and you'll connect them in exciting and unexpected ways.

You'll form these connections when you're dreaming, exercising, meditating, eating, listening to music, in the shower and so on. All you have to do is be open to capturing these connections when they occur to you.

When a connection bubbles to the surface of your mind or when a breakthrough in your side project occurs to you while you're working on your main gig, write it down in your notepad and carry on with your job.

Your subconscious will take care of the rest.

At the very least, use your day-to-day experiences on the job to lend credibility to your art.

American writer Charles Bukowski (1920-1994) spent much of his early life working at a menial job he hated for the United States postal service. He turned many of his experiences on the job into source materials (characters, anecdotes, descriptions) for his breakout 1971 novel *Post Office*.

His protagonist/alter-ego in that story even says while bored on the job, "Maybe I'll write a novel...And then I did."

Organise Your Ideas as You Go

The problem with side projects is you won't always have a lot of free time to work on them.

You must be able to access your research and ideas for your side project quickly and easily. A dedicated file on your computer is a great way to do this. That said, hand-written notes work too.

I keep a file on my computer for each side project, which contains my ideas, conversation snippets, photographs, outlines and more.

When I think of something and don't have access to this file, I write down the thought and put it with the rest of my ideas for my side project at the end of the day.

I also reread each of these ideas at the end of the week to see what I've got.

It takes only a few minutes, but it saves me hours of combing through old research later on.

I feel confident knowing my research is organised and that I can focus on the most important thing – whatever is in front of me.

Kick-start Your Side Project Today

Side projects are the friend of anyone who wants to become more creative and whatever stage you're at in your creative career, they'll help you invest in your future. What you practise for just an hour or two today, could change your life tomorrow – or in seven years.

It took Weiner seven years from the time he started work on his side project until *Mad Men* appeared on our television screens. Weiner's story shows how a side project kept on the back burner can become the main thing over time.

Remember that burnout can happen to you even if you enjoy your job or career. If you feel exhausted, irritable, or cynical about your work, re-invigorate yourself with a side project.

Think of your side project as a long-term investment. Although it might not pay out today or tomorrow, you could reap rewards down the road as Weiner did with *Mad Men*.

If you're a musician in a group, experiment with your solo work in your free time. If you're a nonfiction writer, work on your fiction in the evenings.

If you're a filmmaker for a hit TV show (Congratulations!), work on whatever else inspires you early in the morning or late at night.

What you have on the side today, you'll dine out with tomorrow.

Creative Takeaways

- Start a side project today and give yourself permission to fail.
- Is your main gig turning your hair grey? Take out an old idea, dust it off and play with it a while.

8

GO TO WAR AGAINST YOUR FEARS

"There is only one thing that makes a dream impossible to achieve: the fear of failure."
– Paulo Coelho

IT WASN'T SUPPOSED to be like this.

When you aspired to become an artist, you imagined publishing work that gets better with age and your peers telling each other, "Now there's talent!"

Instead, when you try to create, you feel paralysed.

You don't know if your big idea will survive, and every moment you spend breathing life into it is a struggle.

What you eventually create takes longer than you planned, and it fills you with disappointment.

Here's what happened to me:

When I started writing in public for the first time, I worried how people close to me would react.

What would my friends say if I mined our confidence for a story?

What would my mother think if I wrote about sex?

Will people think I'm odd if I describe how I get up at dawn to write and that I sometimes prefer being alone in a small room with a big idea to the company of others?

I felt like an imposter.

I thought, "*Who are you to call yourself a writer? Get out of here before I call the police!*"

My fears held me back from being honest on the blank page because I was worried about what other people would think.

These selfish fears held me back from my best mistakes, from unexpected opportunities and from becoming a better writer.

I should have written about the party where I drank too much and embarrassed myself, the time I got fired and what happened next.

I should have shown my warts because that's the job. I should have known I was facing one of the common fears everyone with a big idea faces.

I'm Afraid of Starting

Starting is tough.

When I was in my early twenties, I told people I wanted to write a book. What I didn't tell them about was my problem.

For years, I couldn't start writing. I'd open up my word processor and then switch to my internet browser for research. I'd answer my email or see if there was something I wanted to buy on Amazon. Afterwards, I'd check my bank balance and feel depressed.

It went on like this until I disappeared down a rabbit hole of meaningless web searches and doing anything but my most important work.

I wasn't writing anything. I believed I wasn't ready to write, and I needed some anointed mentor to pull me aside and say, "Bryan, now is your time."

Jealous of the success of others and sick of my lack of progress, I joined a fiction and nonfiction writing workshop in Dublin. On the second evening, the instructor said every student had to submit a short story.

I was afraid of starting, but I was even more afraid of being found out.

I hadn't written a short story in years, but I didn't want the class or the instructor to know.

A writer in a writing class who doesn't write, is a fraud.

I went home, and I wrote. I wrote that night and the night after that. I wrote until I finished my first short story. It was terrible – the instructor told me this later – but that didn't matter.

I had taken the first step towards facing my fear of starting.

How to Conquer This Fear

If you're having trouble starting, remember: It's your job to turn up and work on your big idea.

Be brutal with the activities filling your day. No, I'm not suggesting unemployment or divorce. Instead, eliminate the non-essential:

- Quit Facebook.
- Delete the email app from your phone.
- Watch television only on the weekend.
- Turn off notifications on your computer.
- Disable your internet access while you work on your ideas.

Protect your free time and concentrate on developing a habit of creating every day.

I learnt how to start by creating subtle mental triggers for writing. These include brewing coffee, setting a timer for how long I want to write and disconnecting from the internet.

My routine for becoming a writer involves doing this at the same time each evening or morning. It's a ritual, and that means I don't have to think about starting.

To the outsider, this routine looks dull, but it helps me write. Writing is more exciting than anything else I could do with my free time.

Once you've learned how to start, consider it a victory to work on your ideas for 10 minutes without getting distracted. The next day, aim for 15 minutes. The day after, work on your ideas for 20 minutes.

Let these small personal victories accumulate over time and you will conquer this fear. You'll know you're winning when it feels like your ideas are taking over your life. That's a better problem–trust me.

I'm Afraid I'm Not Good Enough

Before writing this series, I published two books: *A Handbook for the Productive Writer* (now called *The Savvy Writer's Guide to Productivity*) and a novella *Poor Brother, Rich Brother*.

I am nobody.

While writing the former, I was afraid others would ask, "What right do you have to explain how to be productive?"

I still think that.

I also knew I'd spent hours researching productivity methods and studying how artists work. I'd read dozens of books by authors explaining how they work, and I knew enough to organise my thoughts into a book.

Even though I am nobody, I gave myself permission to write a book because we've got to start somewhere.

Today, I'm afraid of hugely successful writers like Stephen King, Neil Gaiman and J.K. Rowling. They can write or create far more substantial works per year than I ever could in a lifetime.

King, for example, writes at least one novel per year, and his books are hardly thin. Books like *The Stand* and *The Shining* are more than 500,000 words long, while J.K. Rowling has created an entire world that people have made films about and even created a theme park to bring her fictional world to life.

I wonder, why bother? Shouldn't I just leave things in King's and Rowling's more than talented hands and stop wasting my time?

If you're not a writer, perhaps your negative self-talk goes a little a like this:

- Why can't I think of anything creative?
- I'll never be able to think of a unique idea.
- I'm too old/too young/not talented enough to learn how to play my favourite instrument.
- I'm afraid of performing in public because I'll forget what comes next.

Let's fix that.

How to Conquer This Fear

I'd like to tell you negative self-talk disappears when you're standing on the foundations of experience and success, but even creative masters doubt themselves. The Dutch post-impressionist painter Vincent Van Gogh (1853-1890) struggled with self-doubt throughout his entire life. His advice?

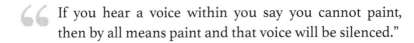 If you hear a voice within you say you cannot paint, then by all means paint and that voice will be silenced."

Become aware of your negative self-talk and listen to it. If your mind is a blue sky, negative self-talk is nothing more than black clouds that you can watch as they pass.

Accept negative self-talk for what it is – just talk. If this is a struggle, ask yourself:

- Was there a trigger that precipitated this negative self-talk?
- Am I looking for affirmation from someone else?
- Can I acknowledge my imperfections for what they are: part of the shared human experience?

Indulge for a few minutes in this self-reflection. Then, set this negative self-talk aside by journaling, meditating or exercising.

Then you should be ready to sit down and do your work. Give yourself permission to create. When it feels difficult or overwhelming, remind yourself every artist must start somewhere and now is your time.

To imagine you are a creative poet, writer or musician is to become that person. So, push forward one word, one idea or one beat at a time.

You're almost there.

I'm Afraid They'll Judge Me

"What will my mother say when she finds out I'm writing about sex?"

"What will my friends think when they catch me describing the world and its ugly imperfections?"

"What will my wife/husband do when they see themselves in my work?"

I don't like writing pieces like this. They're hard work, and they're more personal than a guide or a review. I almost deleted this chapter several times.

What's to enjoy about revealing a job didn't work out, I was lazy, and my work failed?

What must you think of me?

New artists find it difficult to separate their personal lives from their work, and they often regard criticism of their work as a reflection on their character.

Fiction writers, for example, often face a disconcerting moment when they reread a piece and find parts of their personal life scattered on the page.

I'll never forget the first time my wife read a short story I'd submitted into a competition. She asked if she was the woman in the story. I didn't admit it then, but she was right.

How to Conquer This Fear

The judgement of your peers and sometimes of people you trust is an essential part of the creative process if you want to overcome your weaknesses.

American film director Andrew Stanton (b. 1965) – he of *WALL–E* and *Finding Nemo* – tells his team at Pixar studios to "fail early and fail fast."

Stanton and his team rely on critical feedback to adjust problems in their work head-on and to avoid costly mistakes in their films down the road. He says,

> You wouldn't say to somebody who is first learning to play the guitar, 'You better think really hard about where you put your fingers in the guitar neck before you strum, because you only get to strum once and that's it. And if you get that wrong, we're going to move on."

Having your work judged is never easy, but the more you reveal your work to the world, the better you'll get at separating yourself from it.

Then when someone in the know criticises your work, know that it's about your work and not about a personal failing of yours.

I'm Afraid of Finishing

When I was in my mid-twenties, I spent years struggling to finish anything. I wrote dozens of short stories and abandoned them. I thought of articles I wanted to write for newspapers; I researched them and then I never finished them.

There wasn't any one moment when I learnt how to complete my work and become a writer. Instead, I got a job as a journalist writing for a newspaper. There, I had to finish my articles by a deadline because if I didn't my editor would have fired me.

I know this because he called me into his office after I missed a deadline and told me so.

Finishing is harder than starting for another reason too.

Many artists say they feel a certain sense of emptiness when their book, painting, album or big idea is finished. You live with something for hours, days, months or even years, fantasise about the moment it's over and then when that time comes, you feel bereft.

How to Conquer This Fear:

I stopped polishing my articles until they were perfect and I finished them.

On more than one occasion, my editor sent the pieces back to me, saying I'd left out an important paragraph or my introduction needed reworking. Other times, the sub-editors of the paper revised my articles entirely.

Having my work being taken apart felt brutal, but at least I was getting paid to write, and I learnt more from finishing my articles than from endlessly reworking them.

If the finish line feels far away, break your work down into smaller pieces that you can finish one by one. Instead of finishing an album, finish one song. Instead of writing a screenplay, write a scene. Repeat until you finish.

Know that you must break away from your creative project in the end and release it into the world. Then, erect a boundary between who you are as a person and the big idea you've finished.

Actor Johnny Depp (b. 1963) is just one of the many successful actors and actresses who erect such barriers.

 I would rather stay as ignorant as possible about the result of anything because once you're done playing that character, it's really not your business anymore."

Depp, like many writers and musicians who dislike listening to their old works or rereading their novels, doesn't watch himself in past films. Depp like many creative masters stands apart from his big ideas and because of this, he is free to grow in different directions.

I'm Afraid of Failure and Rejection

Most artists have stacks of unpublished essays, articles and stories in their drawer, notebook or on their computer.

Your personal slush pile could be a stack of paintings, recordings or something else entirely. Know that it's all part of the creative process.

Every creative work isn't meant to succeed. Not everything Shakespeare (1564-1616) wrote was a hit. His plays *Troilus and Cressida* and *Timon of Athens*, which he wrote at the height of his creative powers, are far less popular and acclaimed than *Hamlet* and *King Lear*.

Some pieces serve as markers for your journey towards becoming a better artist or as evidence that you're doing the work.

How to Conquer This Fear:

I was rejected more times than I care to admit over the past week. I contacted five authors I admire with interview requests. Four of them said no.

I asked several podcasting experts for their advice for a guest blog post I'm writing. Half of them didn't reply.

I pitched guest posts at three big blogs, two of which said no.

People are going to reject your ideas, and that's OK. Rejection waits for you at the beginning, in the middle and at the end of your big ideas. It goes where you go. Everybody who succeeds gets rejected.

By turning up and creating, you cut through your fear of rejection. Even if some people reject your work, others will embrace it. The next editor or patron you pitch might accept your ideas. You could win the next contest. Your next interview request might be granted.

To become an artist, you must create today. You must create now. You create like your life depends on it.

Because it does.

I'm Afraid of Success

When the World Chess Championship began in 1990, Garry Kasparov (b. 1953) was a success. His opponent at the championship was Kasparov's long-time rival Anatoly Karpov, and the odds were in Kasparov's favour.

The two chess players competed in 24 games over three months, with 12 taking place in New York and 12 in Lyon, France.

Although Kasparov began the competition strongly, he began to commit mistakes. He lost the seventh game and, at the close of the first half of the tournament, the men were tied.

After losing a big game, Kasparov looked fragile and afraid. He was in real danger of losing his world title.

The *New York Times* reported, "Mr Kasparov had lost confidence and grown nervous in New York."

Instead of quitting, Kasparov turned to a secret mental strategy for conquering his fear. When he sat down at the board for a decisive match in France, Kasparov puffed up his chest, and adopted a fiercely aggressive playing style. He acted as if he were confidence itself.

Chess player Josh Waitzkin wrote:

 Everyone in the chess world was afraid of Garry and he fed on that reality. If Garry bristled at the chessboard, opponents would wither. So if Garry was feeling bad, but puffed up his chest, made aggressive moves, and appeared to be the manifestation of Confidence itself, then opponents would become unsettled. Step by step, Garry would feed off his own chess moves, off the created position, and off his opponent's building fear, until soon enough the confidence would become real and Garry would be in flow. He was not being artificial.

Garry was triggering his zone by playing Kasparov chess."

Through acting like a champion, Kasparov subsequently won the sixteenth, eighteenth and twentieth games and retained his title as World Chess Champion.

How to Conquer This Fear

To overcome your fear of success, adopt the Kasparov mind-set. Force yourself to behave like you're full of great ideas; you know what you're doing, and you've already won.

If you're working on a novel and you're afraid of what will happen when you achieve a breakthrough, ask yourself, "How would a great novelist and storyteller write this?"

If you're composing a track for an album and the hook scares you, ask yourself, "How would a world-class musician play this?"

Be bold with your answers. Push past that place of discomfort and fear until you reach a place where your success is inevitable.

Offer no quarter for self-doubt. When you enter into the mental zone that belongs to the victorious, you won't fear success; you'll relish it.

Seizing Victory

Each morning when I sit down in front of the blank page, I feel the heavy paws of fear on my shoulders pressing me down, his cold breath in my ear, his raspy voice telling me, "You're not good enough."

I step forward one word, one sentence, one paragraph, one idea at a time. I force myself to press "Publish" because this is a war I must win. Then, I reach out to others and show them what I've done.

When they don't believe me, I show them my wounds.

Do you know what happened when I did this for the first time?

Nothing.

Our would-be audience is more concerned with the problems in their lives than anything you and I are too afraid to say or to finish.

The problem isn't what people will think of our work or that we're damaged or too ambitious. It's convincing our would-be audience that our big ideas are worth their time.

Go to war against your fears.

If victory were easy, the conquest wouldn't be worth it, but your struggle and frustrations are simply opportunities in disguise. You will unmask them for what they are during your bold march forward.

What you must never do is retreat because filling a blank page or a virgin canvas is too much work.

What you must never do is to let difficult moments overwhelm you and prevent you from seeking out new ways to improve your craft.

What you must never do is quit on a big idea because it's more elusive than you thought.

So create, damn it.

Don't hold back.

And put your ideas out there.

Because each idea you fire is an arrow into the belly of the beast.

Creative Takeaways

- Work on your idea for just 10 minutes today, 15 minutes tomorrow and 20 the day after that. Through the power of small daily wins, you can accomplish more on the blank page or virgin canvas.
- If you haven't accomplished anything in a while, finish just one of your creative projects, however small. Through finishing, you'll discover more about what to create next.

9

LASTING CHANGE, JUST AROUND THE CORNER

"Art is the triumph over chaos."
– John Cheever

IT'S BEEN five years since I turned 30 and picked myself up off the bathroom floor. My beard is more grey, and my hairline has receded further up my head, but I've faced some of my fears.

I long ago left the job I hated. I found another job, lost that one and then moved into a career that rewards me. Outside of work, I push myself to write 1,000 words a day, to publish honest articles and stories on a blog once a week and in books like this one.

These are my choices. Some of them were good, and some were bad, but it's better to move forwards than to be trapped in a rut.

I won't lie, all this honesty and the constant hunt for ideas is a challenge that sometimes leaves me cowering.

I still fall down, face painful mistakes and feel like giving up. Last year instead of publishing a book that was almost ready, I wasted three months rewriting an old book because I was afraid of what I'd written.

When this happens, I lean on my habits.

I don't try to knock out *War and Peace* in a weekend; sometimes writing 500 words is enough. I push forwards until I gain momentum on difficult creative projects.

I practise strengthening my mind and body through meditation and long-distance running because depression, anxiety and ill-health are an anathema to thinking big.

Even if I don't think of a good idea today or tomorrow, I know with the right preparation and a consistent daily practise, I'll find an idea I can use in the end.

I count on these daily habits as ordinary blessings that lead to greater things.

I haven't discovered some ancient secret or transformed myself into a zebra who can magically change its stripes. Instead, I realised that creative masters from the arts, business, technology and more will help us become more creative...if we look hard enough.

Look at how McCartney mined his dreams for songs, how Dali held himself to a routine so he was free to paint or even how Weiner relied on an assistant to help him write while balancing a main job.

We just have to be brave enough to walk the path mapped by these creative masters.

Look, most people believe creativity is a natural ability you either have or lack, but now you and I know to be creative is to embark on a journey that nourishes and strengthens us with every step.

What Your Journey Looks Like

Start by finding out what you feel passionate about.

People say it's a "passion project" when they're describing a film they had to create, a book they were compelled to write or an album they needed to record even though they'd no idea if their work would sell.

If you can find what you feel passionate about, you'll have a reason to get up, get out there and create.

Now don't get me wrong: When you're new at your craft, some

people will wonder what you're doing and how you're spending your time.

It doesn't help that many of your early ideas serve as inward markers of your progress – that you turned up, that you tried – rather than something you can show.

Passion will keep you going when nothing else will. It's your lifeline during dark times. So pay attention to what drives and inspires you, to what you work on in the wee small hours. It's your guiding purpose.

Understand becoming more creative is as much about preparation and smart habits as it is about moments of divine inspiration.

Weiner spent years researching *Mad Men* on the side. Hill lay in bed each night mentally preparing with his imaginary council for the following day. Even Cheever used journal writing as a form of practice.

You'll have more time to prepare and create smart habits if you cull pointless activities from your life. Instead of watching another boxset on Netflix, learn how to ease yourself into your work and nudge yourself forwards, one idea, one side project at a time.

When you're starting off, you might need to support yourself with a "real job" and practise your passion projects around the margins of the day, in the morning before work or late at night.

That's OK.

Your job is a safety net that gives you freedom to learn what your audience wants and your craft demands each day. It gives you the freedom to jump without feeling overwhelmed by fear. Besides, lots of artists worked in other jobs when they were starting off.

T.S. Elliot worked in a bank. Ernest Hemingway was a journalist. Even Leonardo da Vinci took jobs as an advisor to his patrons and king.

If it helps, know that side projects (whether you consider them your job or what you do late at night or first thing in the morning) can lead to great and unexpected things.

I know it's tough.

Some days you will strike the page or canvas repeatedly, but nothing will spark. Your creative work is a grind, you put in hours alone in a room and produce nothing more than a useless sentence, a single chord or a sketch.

Your practise feels like a lonely cry in the dark.

And the reply?

A little voice whispering, *"What do you think you're doing?"*

King heard that same voice when he wrote an early draft of *Carrie*, but his wife helped him finish his first book. He was brave enough to listen to his mentor.

If you've struggled up till now, you too can change your stripes.

Turn up every day and practise your craft, even when you don't feel like it. Acknowledge your fears and self-doubt for what they are: Imposters in the way of your creative ideas.

Push past them!

If you need help practising or you want to save time, pick a creative master to follow. Using their guidance, you can avoid many of the potholes and wrong turns that lie before you.

Remember to be bold with your creative experiments, challenge your assumptions, put one foot in front the other and keep going.

The road ahead is long and winding, but you are bolder, stronger and more powerful than you can imagine.

AFTERWORD

If you enjoyed this book, please rate it and leave a short review. Reviews like yours help me write more books like this one.

Finally, if you have feedback about this book you can always email bryan@becomeawritertoday.com. I'd love to hear from you.

WAIT!
DID YOU WANT BOOK 2 FOR FREE TODAY?

Visit
becomeawritertoday.com/poc

Visit becomeawritertoday.com/poc and I'll send you book two free today.

ACKNOWLEDGMENTS

Thanks to Command+Z Content and Beth Crosby for their great editing and Martine Ellis for proof-reading. Thanks to Terri Black for the book cover design. And finally, thank you for reading.

ABOUT THE AUTHOR

In this life, Bryan Collins is an author.

In another life, he worked as a journalist and a radio producer. Before that, he plucked chickens. He is passionate about helping people accomplish more with their writing projects, and when he's not writing, he's running.

At becomeawritertoday.com, Bryan offers new writers practical advice about writing, creativity, productivity and more. His work has appeared on *Fast Company*, *Lifehacker* and *Copyblogger*.

Bryan holds a degree in communications and journalism, a diploma in social care, a master's degree in disability studies and a diploma in digital media.

You can reach him on Twitter @BryanJCollins, via email at bryan@becomeawritertoday.com or join his Become a Writer Today Facebook page.

Bryan is also the author of the novella *Poor Brother, Rich Brother* and a three-part series: *Become a Writer Today*.

He lives an hour outside of Dublin.

becomeawritertoday.com
bryan@becomeawritertoday.com

TOOLS FOR BECOMING MORE CREATIVE

Below is a list of tools I use and rely on as a writer and blogger.

I've also included some other recommended resources that will help you with your creative work.

The list is relatively long and (depending on the nature of your creative work) you won't need to use all of these tools.

Remember, the creative process and your ideas are more important than any tool.

99designs

In the past, I've used 99designs to find a designer to create a book cover for one of my books. If you want a professional design (like a logo, t-shirt, business card or packaging) for your online business, 99designs is a good place to start.

A smartphone

The best camera is the one you have with you at the time, and if you need to take a picture or just capture an idea, your smartphone is almost always the best choice. I use an iPhone.

A whiteboard

I keep a large whiteboard next to where I write. It's a great way of capturing and organising ideas. I also use it for mind maps and for creating outlines for articles, chapters and even books. I find a whiteboard less confining that traditional digital tools.

Audible

As a creative person, your inputs (what you read, listen to and watch) are just as important as your outputs (what you write, paint or draw). I spend at least an hour a day listening to audiobooks that I purchased from Audible on my smartphone. If you sign up, they'll give you your first audiobook for free.

Behance

A showcase site for design and other creative work. Behance is great for inspiration and also for finding designers to work with. Also, see Dribble.

Brain.FM

Brain.FM provides AI-generated music for focus, relaxation and deep work. When I use this, I find I can enter a state of creative flow faster. Plug in a pair of headphones and you're good to go.

Buffer

I use Buffer to share articles, photos and social media updates by myself and others on Instagram, Facebook, LinkedIn, Twitter and Pinterest. Buffer simplifies sharing social media updates across multiple networks and enables you to schedule your updates in advance.

You can also collaborate with others and enable them to manage your social media profiles... leaving you more time to work on your creative projects. More advanced social media users should consider Meet Edgar.

Canva

For years, I used Photoshop and the rest of the Adobe Suite to create images. Today, I rely on Canva because it simplifies creating images using a drag-and-drop editor.

Creative Commons

This site will help you legally share your work online and find a license or copyright that suits your business model, website or project.

The site's search tool will also help you find images, music and other media that you can use in your creative projects, commercial or otherwise.

Dragon Dictate

I use Dragon software to dictate early drafts of blog posts, book chapters and articles. This piece of software enables me to write faster, and it also reduces the amount of time I spend struggling with repetitive strain injury (RSI). In this article, I explain how to get started with dictation.

Evernote

If I have an idea that I don't want to forget, I keep it in here. I also save articles I like into Evernote as part of my personal swipe file. Sometimes, I take photos of mind maps on my whiteboard with my phone and put them in Evernote too. It's my digital brain.

Image sites

Gratisography contains awesome and free high-resolution photos you can use for your creative projects, as does All The Free Stock and Death to the Stock.

I recommend Depositphotos for premium stock images. You could also take the images yourself and apply an Instagram filter. Designers can get icons on The Noun Project.

Freedom

If you keep getting distracted while writing, use the app Freedom.

It will disable your internet access for a pre-determined period, allowing you to focus on writing and not on cat videos!

Grammarly

If you need help proofing your work, I always recommend you hire a proofreader. However, I also recommend <u>Grammarly</u> as another line of defence and for checking your writing as you go.

Google Docs

I use Google Docs to write on the go and to track my progress in spreadsheets. I also collaborate with other writers and creative professionals, and *it's free*.

G Suite (formerly Google Apps for Work)

It's time to put the hard-drives and USB keys away. Essentially, G Suite enables me to send and receive emails from the Become-AWriterToday.com domain (bryan[at]BecomeAWriterToday.com) using the Gmail interface.

I also get lots of additional cloud storage and can easily collaborate with other writers, editors and designers. This isn't free, but it's affordable.

Headline Analyzer

This free online tool will check your headlines and give you practical tips for improving them so they are more emotional and captivating. Alternatively, consider CoSchedule Headline Analyzer.

Headspace

This is my meditation app of choice. If you've never meditated before, Andy Puddicombe will teach you the basics through guided lessons. I also suggest searching for Tara Brach's free guided meditations online.

Hemingway App

If you're not a confident writer, don't worry. This app will review your text and, in the spirit of Ernest Hemingway, it will tell you what to remove or edit so your writing is bold and clear.

Kindle Spy

KindleSpy is a great tool that will help you see which books are selling on Amazon and how much they earn. Then you can use this information to increase sales of your book.

LeadPages

I use LeadPages to create landing and squeeze pages for my books. I also use it to create sign-up forms for my mailing list.

Your bed or chair of choice

Fact: Napping is conducive to creativity. Just ask Salvador Dali. The trick is to wake yourself up after 20 minutes so you avoid going into a deep sleep. Then when you wake, get straight to work.

Noise cancelling headphones and an album of instrumental music

A good set of noise cancelling headphones will help you concentrate on your work no matter where you are. Each morning, I don my pair and listen to albums like "Rain for Sleeping and Relaxation" on repeat while I write.

(Yes, that album is exactly like the name sounds.)

iMindMap/MindNode/MindMeister

I've used these affordable tools to create mind maps in the past. They're easy to learn too. Alternatively, you can create a mind map using pen and paper.

Medium

Do you just want to write and share your ideas online, but you're not interested in running a blog? Medium removes all of the technical challenges of blogging and helps you connect with readers.

Oblique Strategies

In 1975, the producer and musician Brian Eno and the artist and painter Peter Schmidt created a deck of cards that give musicians and artists constraints within which to work.

These constraints foster the kind of lateral thinking creativity demands. Essentially, you draw a card at random from the deck and are presented with a prompt like: 'Do the words need changing?'

You can buy the deck or use a free, web-version.

Pilot G4 Pen and a Moleskine notebook

No, there's no need to use a Moleskine notebook for writing or capturing ideas, but I'm drawn to the build quality of these notebooks and the feel of the paper. I've a box full of these near where I write.

Even if you're not drawn to these admittedly expensive notebooks, working on your ideas with a pen (you can't go wrong with the Pilot G4) and paper will liberate fresh thinking.

Screenflow for Mac

This is a great tool for recording video and screencasts. It's also relatively simple to edit your recordings and export them to a format suitable for Facebook, YouTube or your website. Also consider Camtasia.

Scrivener

I can't recommend Scrivener enough. I use it to write blog posts and books. I've used Scrivener to write feature articles for newspapers, reports, ebooks, a thesis and even a novel.

>> Get my free blogging template.

Other useful writing apps include Ulysses, Pages and IA Writer.

Sumo

Sumo is an all-in-one tool that enables you to gather email addresses, set up a share bar on the side of blog posts and also track how people interact with your work online. If you're sharing your work online, I highly recommended it.

Upwork

No matter how talented or hard-working you are, it's impossible to do everything alone. UpWork is a great service for finding designers, editors and more who can help you with time-consuming tasks so you can spend more time on your book, art or music.

I've used Upwork to hire video-editors and developers who fixed problems on my website.

Web-hosting

For your author website or blog, I suggest hosting with Siteground. If you need help, check out my detailed guide on how to start a blog: https://becomeawritertoday.com/start-a-blog/

GET THE POWER OF CREATIVITY SERIES

Learning How to Build Lasting Habits, Face Your Fears and Change
Your Life
(Book 1)

An Uncommon Guide to Mastering Your Inner Genius and Finding
New Ideas That Matter
(Book 2)

How to Conquer Procrastination, Finish Your Work and Find Success
(Book 3)

http://thepowerofcreativitybook.com

GET THE BECOME A WRITER TODAY SERIES

Yes, You Can Write!
101 Proven Writing Prompts that Will Help You Find Creative Ideas
Faster for Your Journal, Blogging, Writing Your Book and More
(Book 1)

The Savvy Writer's Guide to Productivity
How to Work Less, Finish Writing Your Story or Book, and Find the
Success You Deserve
(Book 2)

The Art of Writing a Non-Fiction Book
An Easy Guide to Researching, Creating, Editing, and Self-Publishing
Your First Book
(Book 3)

http://becomeawritertodaybook.com

REFERENCES

Books

Altucher, James. *Choose Yourself,* James Altucher, 2013.

Bales, David and Orland, Ted. *Art and Fear.* Image Continuum Press. 2001.

Campbell Joseph and Moyers, Bill. *The Power of Myth*, Anchor Books. 1998.

Catmull, Ed. *Creativity Inc.: Overcoming The Unforeseen Forces That Stand in the Way of True Inspiration*. Random House. 2014.

Csikzentmihalyi, Mihaly. *Flow: The Psychology of Happiness.* Ebury Publishing, 2002.

Covey, Stephen R. *The 7 Habits of Highly Effective People.* Free Press. 1989.

Dali, Salvador. *50 Secrets of Magic Craftsmanship.* Dover Publications. 1992.

De Bono, Edward. *How to Have a Beautiful Mind.* Ebury Press. 2008.

Duhigg, Charles. *The Power of Habit: Why We Do What We Do In Life and Business*. Random House. 2012.

Ferriss, Timothy. *Tools of Titans: The Tactics, Routines, and Habits of*

Billionaires, Icons, and World-Class Performers. Ebury Publishing. Kindle Edition. 2016.

Gelb, Michael. *How To Think Like Leonardo da Vinci: Seven Steps to Boosting Your Everyday Genius.* Harper Collins. 2009.

Gladwell, Malcolm. *Outliers: The Story of Success.* Back Bay Books. 2011.

Godin, Seth. *Tribes.* Hachette Digital. 2008.

Godin, Seth. *All Marketers Are Liars.* Portfolio. 2012.

Green, Robert. *Mastery.* Viking. 2012.

Gregoire, Carolyn and Kaufmann, Scott Barry. *Wired to Create: Unraveling the Mysteries of the Creative Mind.* TarcherPerigee. 2015.

Harris, Sam. *Waking Up: A Guide to Spirituality Without Religion.* Simon & Schuster. 2014.

Isaacson, Walter. *Einstein: His Life and Universe.* Simon & Schuster. 2008.

Isaacson, Walter. *Steve Jobs: The Exclusive Biography.* Machete Digital. 2011.

Kahneman, Daniel. *Thinking, Fast and Slow.* Farrer, Straus and Giroux. 2011.

King, Stephen. *On Writing Well: A Memoir of the Craft.* Hodder and Stoughton. 2010.

Kleon, Austin. *Show Your Work.* Workman Publishing Company. 2014.

Kleon, Austin. *Steal Like an Artist.* Workman Publishing Company. 2012.

Levy, Mark. *Accidental Genius: Using Writing to Generate Your Best Ideas, Insight and Content* (Second Edition). Berrett-Koehler Publishers. 2009.

Newport, Cal. *Deep Work: Rules for Focus in a Distracted World.* Piatkus. 2016.

Rodriguez, Robert. *Rebel Without a Crew.* Plume. 1995.

Reis, Eric. *The Lean Startup: How Today's Entrepreneurs Use Continuous Innovation to Create Radically Successful Businesses.* Crown Business. 2011.

Segal, Zoe Gillian. *Getting There.* Harry N. Abrams. 2015.

Tharp, Twyla. *The Creative Habit: Learn It and Use It For Life.* Simon & Schuster. 2014.

T.S. Eliot. *The Sacred Wood: Essays on Poetry and Criticism.* Bartleby.com. 2009.

Waitzkin, Josh. *The Art of Learning: An Inner Journey to Optimal Performance.* Free Press. 2007.

Wilboue, Edwin Charles. *Victor Hugo By A Witness Of His Life.* 2007. Accessed at https://archive.org/stream/victorhugobyawit003274mbp/victorhugoby awit003274mbp_djvu.txt on March 15, 2016

Audio, Videos and Films

The American Reader. *This Day In Lettres: 3 April (1855): Charles Dickens to Maria Winter.* Accessed at http://theamericanreader.com/3-april-1855-charles-dickens-to-maria-winter/ on May 22, 2016.

Cleese, John. *Lecture On Creativity for Video Arts.* 1991. Accessed at https://www.youtube.com/watch?v=Qby0ed4aVpo on November 22, 2015.

Ferris, Tim. *The "Wizard" of Hollywood, Robert Rodriguez.* Four Hour Work Week. 2015. Accessed at The Tim Ferris Experiment http://fourhourworkweek.com/2015/08/23/the-wizard-of-hollywood-robert-rodriguez/ on November 22, 2015.

Greenberg, Robert. *Great Masters: Mozart-His Life and Music.* The Great Courses. 2013.

Pink, Daniel. *The Puzzle of Motivation.* 2009. Accessed at TED http://www.ted.com/talks/dan_pink_on_motivation/transcript?language=en on November 22, 2015.

Lasseter, John et al. *Toy Story.* Pixar Studios. 1995.

Lasseter, John et. al. *Toy Story 2.* Pixar Studios. 2000.

Lucas, George et al. *Star Wars: A New Hope.* Lucasfilm. 1977.

Kershner, Irvin et al. *Star Wars: The Empire Strikes Back.* Lucasfilm. 1980.

Jobs, Steve. *iPhone 2007 Presentation (Full HD).* Accessed at

https://www.youtube.com/watch?v=vN4U5FqrOdQ   on   December
4. 2015.

Articles, Research Papers and Essays

Altmann, E. M. & Trafton, J.G. *Task interruption: Resumption lag and the role of cues.* Department of Psychology. Michigan State University. 2004.

Asimov, Isaac. *How Do People Get New Ideas? MIT Technology review.* 2014. Accessed at https://www.technologyreview.com/s/531911/isaac-asimov-asks-how-do-people-get-new-ideas/ on April 17, 2016.

Baird, Benjamin et. al. *Inspired by Distraction: Mind Wandering Facilitates Creative Incubation.* Psychological Science. 2011. Accessed at http://pss.sagepub.com/content/early/2012/08/31/0956797612446024.abstract on May 9, 2016.

Brogan, Jan. *When being distracted is a good thing.* The Boston Globe. 2012. Accessed at https://www.bostonglobe.com/lifestyle/health-wellness/2012/02/27/when-being-distracted-good-thing/1AYWPlDplqluMEPrWHe5sL/story.html on May 22, 2016.

Clear, James. *The Akrasia Effect: Why We Don't Follow Through on What We Set Out to Do (And What to Do About It).* 2016. Accessed at http://jamesclear.com/akrasia on March 15, 2016.

Coyle, Danie. *A Gauge for Measuring Effective Practice.* The Talent Code. Daniel, Coyle. 2009. Accessed at http://thetalentcode.com/2011/05/31/a-gauge-for-measuring-effective-practice/ on May 9, 2016.

Dumas D, Dunbar KN. *The Creative Stereotype Effect.* PLOS. 2016. Accessed at http://journals.plos.org/plosone/article?id=10.1371/journal.pone.0142567 on May 22, 2016.

Ericsson, Anders K. et al. *The Role of Deliberate Practice in Acquisition of Expert Performance.* American Psychology Association. 1993.

Howie, Hugh. *My advice to aspiring authors.* The Way Finder. 2013.

Accessed at http://www.hughhowey.com/my-advice-to-aspiring-authors/ on June 24, 2016.

Kageyama, Noa. *The Most Valuable Lesson I Learned from Playing the Violin*. The Creativity Post. 2012. Accessed at http://www.creativitypost.com/arts/the_most_valuable_lesson_i_learn ed_from_playing_the_violin on May 22, 2016.

Kelly, Kevin. *1,000 True Fans*. The Technium. 2008. Accessed at http://kk.org/thetechnium/1000-true-fans/ on June 24, 2016.

Herbert, Wray. *Ink on Paper: Some Notes on Note Taking*. Association for Psychological Science. 2014. Accessed at http://www.psychologicalscience.org/index.php/news/were-only-human/ink-on-paper-some-notes-on-note-taking.html on May 22, 2016.

Mac Kinnon, Donald. *The Identification of Creativity*. Applied Psychology. 1963.

Mueller, Pam and Oppenheimer, Daniel. *The Pen Is Mightier Than the Keyboard: Advantages of Longhand Over Laptop Note Taking*. 2014. Accessed at https://sites.udel.edu/victorp/files/2010/11/Psychological-Science-2014-Mueller-0956797614524581-1uoh0yu.pdf on May 22, 2016. Association for Psychological Science.

Oakley, Keith and Djikic, Maja. *How Reading Transforms Us*. New York Times. 2014. Accessed at *http://www.nytimes.com/2014/12/21/opinion/sunday/how-writing-transforms-us.html?_r=0* on September 15, 2015.

Reader's Digest. *The Charles Goodyear Story*. Good Year. 1957. Accessed at *Good Year Corporate*. Accessed at *https://corporate.goodyear.com/en-US/about/history/charles-goodyear-story.html* on November 22, 2015.

Reis, Eric. *How DropBox Started As A Minimal Viable Product*. 2011. Accessed at http://techcrunch.com/2011/10/19/dropbox-minimal-viable-product/ on April 17, 2016.

Schwartz and Porath. *Why You Hate Work*. The New York Times. 2014. Accessed at http://www.nytimes.com/2014/06/01/opinion/sunday/why-you-hate-work.html on February 22, 2016.

Sternberg, Jacques. *In Act 2, the TV Hit Man Becomes a Pitch Man.* The New York Times. 2007. Accessed at http://www.nytimes.com/2007/07/18/arts/television/18madm.html?_r=0 on May 22, 2016.

Walker, Tim. *The Telegraph. Ernest Hemingway never wrote drunk, says granddaughter Mariel Hemingway.* The Telegraph. 2013. Accessed at http://www.telegraph.co.uk/culture/books/booknews/10236200/Ernest-Hemingway-never-wrote-drunk-says-granddaughter-Mariel-Hemingway.html on September 15, 2015.

Wilson, Timothy D et al. *Just think: The challenges of the disengaged mind.* Science Mag. 2014.

Vaynerchuk, Gary. *3 Ways You Need To Be Marketing Your Book in 2015.* Gary Vaynerchuk. 2016. Accessed at https://www.garyvaynerchuk.com/3-ways-you-need-to-be-marketing-your-book-in-2015/ on June 24, 2016.

Ying, Jon. *Meet the Team! (Part 1).* Dropbox, 2009. Accessed at https://blogs.dropbox.com/dropbox/2009/02/meet-the-team-part-1/ on June 24, 2016.